COLLINS GEM

BASIC FACTS

COMPUTERS

B Samways BSc MBCS
and T Byrne-Jones

HarperCollins*Publishers*

HarperCollins Publishers
PO Box, Glasgow G4 0NB, Scotland

First published 1983
Revised edition 1988
Third edition 1991

Reprint 10 9 8 7 6 5 4 3 2 1

ISBN 0 00 459250 6 (UK edition)
    0 00 459251 4 (Export edition)

Printed in Great Britain by
HarperCollins Manufacturing, Glasgow

Introduction

Collins Gem *Basic Facts* is a series of illustrated GEM dictionaries in important school subjects. This new edition has been extensively revised and updated to widen the coverage of the subject and to reflect recent changes in the way it is taught in the classroom.

Bold words in an entry identify key terms which are explained in greater detail in entries of their own; important terms which do not have separate entries are shown in *italic* and are explained in the entry in which they occur.

Other titles in the series include:

Gem *Basic Facts Mathematics*
Gem *Basic Facts Chemistry*
Gem *Basic Facts Physics*
Gem *Basic Facts Science*
Gem *Basic Facts Biology*
Gem *Basic Facts History*
Gem *Basic Facts Geography*
Gem *Basic Facts Craft, Design & Technology*
Gem *Basic Facts Business Studies*

A

abacus One of the earliest counting devices, used for addition and subtraction. It consists of a frame holding rods on which a specific number of beads are free to move. It has 10 balls or beads in each row if working in **denary notation**. Multiplication and division are carried out by repeated addition and subtraction, as in **calculators** and computers today. Another similarity is that it stores the result as well as doing the calculation. An advanced type of abacus is still

(431−9)   (430−8)   (422)

abacus The steps in calculating 431−9. Note that 10 beads on one row can be exchanged for one bead on the row above at any time during the calculation.

used in parts of China as a cheap, easy-to-use calculating device and is very fast in the hands of an expert.

abort   To stop the running of a computer **program**, usually when things go wrong. The computer returns to the **operating system** after aborting the program, prints a message to warn the operator and waits for a new **command**.

absolute address   See **address**.

access time   1. The time taken by the computer to fetch **data** from an **address** within the computer or other storage device.
2. The time between being told to fetch and having the data ready.

accumulator   A special **location** used to hold the result of calculations during processing. A number can be passed to the accumulator, and if a further **instruction** is then given to add another number to it, this will be done and the result again held in the accumulator in place of the previous one. The contents of the accumulator can also be transferred back to the central **memory** or **output** to a **peripheral**.

For example, a program in **machine code** designed to add two numbers together would carry out the arithmetic with three instructions:
(a) Clear accumulator;

(b) Transfer a number to the accumulator, e.g. 37;

(c) Add a second number to that already held by the accumulator, e.g. 48; the accumulator now holds the result, 85.

See **register**.

acronym A word formed from the initial letters of a group of words or a phrase. The world of computing uses many acronyms. For example, there is a **program** whose proper name is 'Beginners' All-purpose Symbolic Instruction Code' but it is much easier to use its acronym **BASIC**. There is a list of common computing acronyms at the end of this book.

adder A device which performs addition on **digital signals** giving both the sum and the **carry digit**. A **half-adder** has two inputs whereas a **full-adder** has three inputs, each input being a 0 or 1.

For example, when adding two binary numbers together electronically, the first column on the right can be dealt with by a half-adder but the other columns require a full-adder as there is a carry digit from the previous column.

$$
\begin{array}{r}
1001101 \\
+0110111 \\
\hline
10000100
\end{array}
$$

address The reference number given to each **location** in a computer's **memory** that stores **data**. Whenever a computer is asked to find a piece of data it has stored it uses the address.

For example,

address	contents
140	C
141	A
142	T
143	255

Address 142 holds the letter T, though both would be stored in **binary notation**. Just as the word CAT is held in three locations so more than one location can be used to hold a number.

The *absolute address* is the number given to each address by the **hardware** when we program using a **low-level language**. This is distinct from *indirect addressing* where the address in one program instruction refers to another location which contains another address. It can be thought of as similar to visiting Tony by calling on Brian first and asking where Tony lives. It is often used by programmers as *relative addressing* to access a series of addresses with just one instruction whose address is increased by one each time it is carried out. It would be similar to calling on a group of neighbours who live next door to one another. For example, a programming instruction might say 'Recall the number stored in the location whose address is given in location XXX'. What is stored in location XXX is then increased by one each time it is recalled.

address bus A major route (a set of wires) along which signals travel to reach a particular **address**. **Data** can then be put into or taken from that address along the **data bus**.

address modification The process by which the **address** part of a **program** instruction is changed, say to one higher (i.e. the next address) each time the instruction is performed. This is very useful if a series of inputs are to be placed in consecutive addresses.

Aiken, Howard (1900–73) American mathematician and computer pioneer. He realized the importance of **Babbage's** analytical engine and suggested the Automatic Sequence Controlled Calculator (ASCC) which, built in the mid-1940s, was the first automatic computer. The program instructions were supplied to this electromechanical machine on paper tape.

ALGOL (acronym for ALGorithmic Oriented Language) A high-level programming **language** developed in Europe at the same time as FORTRAN was being developed in the United States. ALGOL-60 is a problem-solving language designed for mathematical and scientific use, whereas ALGOL-68 is an even more powerful language designed in 1968 for a variety of uses. See **high-level language, algorithm**.

algorithm   A planned set of **instructions** or steps designed to solve a particular problem. There is only one starting point and all routes through the algorithm end at the same finishing point. Such steps can be carried out by a computer, or **dry run** on paper, using different inputs or values.

allocate   See **assign**.

alphanumeric code   A set of **characters** consisting of the letters A to Z and numbers 0 to 9. An alphanumeric keyboard layout is shown below. See **QWERTY**.

```
(1)  (2)  (3)  (4)  (5)  (6)  (7)  (8)  (9)  (0)
   (Q)  (W)  (E)  (R)  (T)  (Y)  (U)  (I)  (O)  (P)
     (A)  (S)  (D)  (F)  (G)  (H)  (J)  (K)  (L)
        (Z)  (X)  (C)  (V)  (B)  (N)  (M)
```

alphanumeric code   An alphanumeric keyboard layout.

analogue   A quantity which changes continuously rather than in jumps, e.g. temperature, speed. In order to record such values in a digital computer, readings are taken at intervals which might be very short such as every microsecond, though could be each hour or each day. The conversion from continuous change to particular values is done by a suitable **analogue-digital converter**.

analogue computer A machine designed to work on **data** which is represented by some physical quantity which varies continuously (unlike digital signals which are 0s and 1s).

For example, the turning of a wheel or changes in voltage can be used as input. Analogue computers are said to operate in **real time** because they respond as things happen and are widely used for research in design where many different shapes and speeds can be tried out quickly. A computer model of a car suspension allows the designer to see the effects of changing size, stiffness and damping.

analogue-digital converter (ADC) A device that is able to convert a continuously varying **signal**, such as voltage, into a series of numbers. It does this by sampling the voltage at regular intervals (say 10 times a second) and changing its **digital output** accordingly.

For example, when a computer is used to switch on and off a heating system it must be able to measure the temperature. Electrical thermometers provide varying voltages (**analogue**) which have to be converted into a series of **digits** (a **binary** number) for the computer.

ancestral file   A previous version of the file that is held to minimize the effect of losing or corrupting **data**. Correct procedure ensures that three copies of a file are kept: grandparent, parent and child; the **disk** accepting the latest version is the child. Next session this disk loads its data into the computer and that version becomes the parent when at the end the updated file is saved as the new child. The parent in turn becomes the grandparent. Should one disk become damaged the operator can continue with the next copy knowing that there is still a third copy. If there were only two copies and the first was damaged, then the second would have to be duplicated on to another disk before being **updated** and this could result in the updated records being lost whilst the second disk is being copied. The third copy is always stored separately from the first two. In practice additional copies are also kept over a period of time.

AND gate   This is a logic gate which operates with **binary digits**. Its output is of logic value 1 only when all its inputs have a logic value 1.

For example, with a two-input AND gate the **truth table** shown below applies. This could be used to find the **carry digit** when two binary digits are added together as there is a carry of 1 only when the two digits to be added are both 1s.

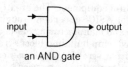

an AND gate

Input		Output
0	0	0
0	1	0
1	0	0
1	1	1

AND gate   Truth table showing the range of possible output values from a two-input AND gate.

applications package   A **program** or set of programs, with user manuals and documentation, written to carry out a particular task. For example, a wages payroll package, a warehouse-control program, or a program controlling a robot welder.

application specific integrated circuits (ASICS)   Customized **chips** developed for manufacturers of other products. Sometimes called *dedicated chips*, these may be used for controlling a particular task, for example, washing-machine programs, speech-recognition chips, or the operation of modern hi-fi equipment. The greatly increased popularity of ASICS has been brought about by new design and manufacturing methods based on standardized chip-building blocks rather than designing from scratch, which has enabled the costs of development to be reduced.

archived file   A type of file kept, for example, on magnetic tape and which has to be loaded on to the disk or tape drive when required. It is not kept permanently in the computer and so does not take up valuable space.

argument   A variable factor, the value of which sets the value of the function of which it is part. For example, to find the square root when programming in **BASIC** we use a function such as SQR(X). The output value of this function is governed by the value of the argument X.

arithmetic logic unit (ALU)   The part of the computer where the calculations are carried out (addition and subtraction) and the logic operations are performed. The **ALU** is part of the **central processing unit** and has a **memory** store for holding the results of calculations while processing is going on (see opposite).

array   An arranged set of **locations** any of which can be accessed from a common starting **address**, or **identifier**, rather than individually.

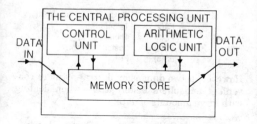

arithmetic logic unit

For example, consider a block of flats having eight floors with four flats on each floor. The flats could be numbered (coded) 1 to 32 as in a one-dimensional array and referred to as FLAT 1, FLAT 2 etc. Alternatively they could be numbered 11 to 14 on the first level, 21 to 24 on the second level, 31 to 34 on the third level as in a two-dimensional array and referred to as LEVEL 2 ROOM 3 etc. (Note that when using rows and columns an item of **data** is always accessed by the row and then the column). If the names of the people who live in the flats are Oakley, Talbot, Thomas, Foster, Fish, Simmons, Selby, Ellis, Nelson and so on, then these names could be stored in a one-dimensional array F\$1, F\$2, F\$3, etc. (In **BASIC** the \$ signifies a **string**):

F$(1)	Oakley
F$(2)	Talbot
F$(3)	Thomas
F$(4)	Foster
F$(5)	Fish

However, a two-dimensional array is more convenient and offers faster access when dealing with large amounts of data:

1st level	Oakley	Talbot	Thomas	Foster
2nd level	Fish	Simmons	Selby	Ellis

To obtain the names of those living at the seventh level we would use references F$(7,1), F$(7,2), F$(7,3) and F$(7,4).

artificial intelligence (AI) The ability a machine has to learn from its experiences and to make decisions based on these experiences, rather like a human being. For example, a machine may play chess, but if each time it plays it learns from its mistakes and plays better the next time, then it is said to have artificial intelligence.

ASCII code (acronym for American Standard Code for Information Interchange — pronounced 'ASKEY') A standard code used for the transmission of data, particularly the exchange of data between machines. Many manufacturers design their own codes for their machines but ASCII code is often used as a standard thus enabling link-ups between various computers and **peripherals** such as **printers**.

0	48	C	67	O	79	a	97
1	49	D	68	P	80	b	98
2	50	E	69	Q	81	c	99
3	51	F	70	R	82	d	100
4	52	G	71	S	83	e	101
5	53	H	72	T	84	space	32
6	54	I	73	U	85	!	33
7	55	J	74	V	86	*	42
8	56	K	75	W	87	+	43
9	57	L	76	X	88	−	45
A	65	M	77	Y	89	/	47
B	66	N	78	Z	90	=	61

ASCII code

aspect ratio The ratio of the width of a television **screen** to the height. 4:3 has been adopted by the United Kingdom and many other countries though there are plans to introduce a longer letter-box shape which could have additional pictures at the side or cope with the wider picture used by cinema films.

assembly language A **low-level language** which is similar to the way in which the computer **hardware** works but is easier to use than **machine code** for programming. The computer manufacturer provides an assembler and this **program** translates the completed assembly language program into machine code, one programming instruction becoming one machine code instruction.

assign 1. To reserve part of the computing system, e.g. the **printer**, for use by a **program** during its running. Note that to **allocate** is similar but is controlled during the running and may make the particular **hardware** available to other programs at certain times.
2. Assign is also used by some **operating systems** as a **command** that allows all references to a particular **disk** drive to go to another one.

astable Continually switching (*oscillating*) from one state to the other, describing an electronic device used for timing in electronic watches and as the basis for the computer **clock**.

asynchronous mode The way in which a computer works whereby the end of one operation allows the start of the next. The machine does not have to wait for the next clock cycle to start each operation, as in **synchronous mode**.

Atlas The best-known of the **second generation** computers which were built using **tran-**

sistors as opposed to the thermionic valves of the **first generation**.

audit trail A record provided by some business and financial **software** of all the transactions that have taken place during previous amendments to **data** in order that subsequent checking may take place.

author language A programming **language** which allows the inexperienced user to compose a learning sequence including the use of **multimedia**. For example, Microtext is an author language specially developed for **computer-assisted learning** packages (CAL).

automated teller machine (ATM) A computerized cash dispenser which accepts cash-cards.

auto-start A code stored in a **read only memory (ROM)** in some commercial microcomputers. In such cases, on switching on, this automatically loads, say, the **operating system** and/or an **interpreter** and an **applications package** into the machine which is then immediately ready to use. **Turnkey** is a term often used to describe this facility.

B

Babbage, Charles (1791–1871) English mathematician who saw the need for an accurate calculating device and tried to build a 'difference engine'. In 1833 he proposed the *analytical engine* which in principle was the forerunner of today's computer. Using punched cards it was designed to perform calculations automatically and was the first type of digital computer.

backing store A store for large amounts of **data** which can be transmitted easily (though not always quickly) to the **main store** when required. It also has the advantage of being a non-**volatile memory**. Examples are magnetic cards or magnetic disks.

backup A spare copy for when things go wrong and to avoid the disaster which can follow the damaging or corruption of **disks** or **data**. All users should have at least one duplicate copy or backup of their **program** or data though more would be advisable. The **ancestral file** method offers additional **security** for data.

bar code   A set of lines of varying widths which can be read by passing a **light pen** across them. On household goods there are 30 lines giving a unique 13-digit code number to each product. When the cashier records this number, the machine finds the price from **memory** and is able to register that there is now one less of that item in stock. Library cards and library books sometimes have bar codes, though with more lines. Here the borrowing of books during the day is recorded on to **tape** by means of a light pen and the **data** is transferred to the computer at the end of the day.

country code · manufacturer's code · product code

bar code

BASIC (acronym for Beginner's All-purpose Symbolic Instruction Code)   A **high-level language** used for general or conversational programming. Developed by Kemeny and Kurtz in

1964 in the USA, it was originally designed for educational use as an easy-to-learn language. Students could input their programs one line at a time, each of which would be checked by the computer before the next one was accepted.

batch processing The system of collecting all the different inputs or **programs** together and putting them into a computer in one set or batch. This only involves the operator in 'one' loading and running operation no matter how many programs are in the batch. The programs are processed as a single unit thus avoiding wasted computer time as each program is loaded. Job control cards control each program while it is processed.

For example, in a school without its own computing facilities each pupil in a class could write a program on **mark sense cards** which can be taken and fed, on batch, to a distant computer. Not only would there usually be a delay before these could be run but several days could pass before the **output** is returned.

batch total See **hash total**.

baud rate The number of **bits** per second transmitted along a wire. Originally it was based on the speeds of transmitting Morse code. Named after the French inventor, J.M.E. Baud (1845–1903).

Rate	Used by
110 baud	Teletype terminal to computer
300 baud	Slow-speed cassette tape to micro
1200 baud	Prestel set receiving data
7000000 baud	Data transfer by satellites
1000 million baud	Possible speed with optic fibre

baud rate   Examples of common baud rates.

benchmark   A **program** task which is given to different makes of computers to measure their performance and thus allows us to compare one with another.

binary coded decimal (BCD)   To be able to change any of our numbers 0 to 9 into binary, we require up to four **binary digits**. The coding system BCD uses four binary digits for each decimal number. But note that with four binary digits numbers up to 15 can be coded in this way. The final six numbers are coded as letters in the **hexadecimal** system (see table overleaf).

binary digit   One of the two digits used in **binary notation**, either a 0 or 1.

binary fractions   Each **binary digit** has twice the value of the one on its right whether it comes

denary	binary	hex
0	0000	0
1	0001	1
2	0010	2
3	0011	3
4	0100	4
5	0101	5
6	0110	6
7	0111	7
8	1000	8
9	1001	9
10	1010	A
11	1011	B
12	1100	C
13	1101	D
14	1110	E
15	1111	F

binary coded decimal

before or after the bicimal point. For example,
11.11 in binary represents

$$2+1+0.5+0.25$$

that is, 3.75 in **denary**.

binary notation In this system numbers are
represented by the two digits 0 and 1, i.e. base 2.
When we count in tens (base 10) each digit is 10
times the value of the one on its right. In binary
(base 2) each digit has twice the value.

Binary	Denary		Binary	Denary
0	0		101	5
1	1		110	6
10	2		111	7
11	3		1000	8
100	4		1001	9

binary notation   Examples of binary numbers and their denary equivalents.

value	16		8		4		2		1	
binary	1		0		0		1		1	
denary	16	+	0	+	0	+	2	+	1	= 19

binary notation   10011 in binary is 19 in denary.

Binary uses the same rules as for denary arithmetic but in twos instead of tens as shown overleaf.

Because binary notation has only two digits, it can be easily represented electronically by two voltage levels and can be stored in any system having two states. For these reasons it is used by computers.

$$\begin{array}{r} 0010 \\ +1011 \\ \hline \end{array}$$

$$\begin{array}{r} 1101 \\ -0110 \\ \hline \end{array}$$

(a)   1101   (b)   0111

binary notation Examples of (a) binary addition and (b) binary subtraction.

bistable Having two states, referring to an electronic device and forming the basis of a computer **memory**. In one state it can be considered to represent a 0 and in the other state a 1.

bit One of the two digits 0 and 1 used in **binary notation**. The word comes from **BI**nary digi**T**.

bit pattern The arrangement of **bits** within a word representing a **character** or **instruction**. For example, 01000101 is the bit pattern for an upper case E in the **ASCII** code.

black box A concept used to show how units go together to make a system without having to explain the workings of the individual units (see diagram opposite).

BLAISE Acronym for the British Library Automated Information Service.

block A set of records, figures or words which are treated by the computer as a single unit of

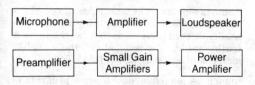

black box A public address system may be represented by three boxes (top). The amplifier itself may be represented as a further three boxes (bottom).

data. For example, **microcomputer** data is transferred to and from a cassette **tape** recorder in blocks. These blocks are sometimes indicated by numbers on the **screen** though they can be distinctly heard by just playing the tape.

block diagram A diagram used to help explain a system, this consists of labelled boxes joined by lines with arrows similar to a **program flow-chart**. It is used for systems such as electrical circuits. See **black box**.

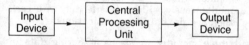

block diagram A block diagram of a simple computer system.

Boolean algebra The set of rules allowing logical statements to be written using algebra. The results of such statements can be shown in a **truth table**. Named after the English mathematician George Boole (1815–64).

branch A jump from one step in a **program** to a different part indicated by a branch **instruction**. For example, a conditional branch might depend on the value of something at that time, i.e. 'branch if the value of X is greater than 7'.

breadboard An experimental circuit board which is used to try out possible circuits. Often included on a **microprocessor** learning/teaching kit for **interfacing** and **control technology**.

BREAK key This key allows the user to stop the computer; usually the result is that the contents of the temporary **memory** are lost. It is not available on all computers.

broadband A transmission technique which uses a wide range of frequencies to allow telecommunications messages to be sent simultaneously without interfering with each other. See also **data communications**.

bubble memory A means of storing **data** in **binary notation**. Small cylinders of magnetism, called bubbles, are created and held stationary by magnets in an **integrated circuit** (or **chip**) made from magnetic material. Each bubble is used to represent a 1 whereas the absence of a bubble indicates a 0. To keep the bubbles in place chevrons are put on the surface of the chip (shown V-shaped). Bubbles are created at one end, moved by magnetic fields (not shown in diagram) across the chip as required and read in sequence. Thus it is a **serial access memory** but has the advantage of being non-**volatile** and capable of high density storage. This whole book could be stored as 0s and 1s on four bubble memory chips each less than a square centimetre.

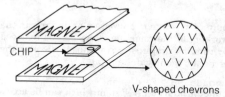

V-shaped chevrons

bubble memory

bubble sort   A routine for sorting items into an order, e.g. from the highest to the lowest. Starting at the top of a list the **program** compares each **data** item with the next and moves it up the list if appropriate (rising like a bubble). This process is repeated over and over again until there is no movement during a complete pass through, and all the items have 'bubbled' into their right place.

buffer A temporary **store** for **data** which is being transferred, generally used to allow for a difference in speeds.

For example, what is typed on a **microcomputer keyboard** is generally held in a buffer until the return or **ENTER key** is pressed. Many **printers** have buffers that are filled with what is to be printed at a much faster rate than the actual printing.

bug A mistake in a program or an error in the working of the computer. Bugs can be removed by running **diagnostic routines** to discover the error and then by **debugging**.

bulletin boards A system which can be accessed by a computer with a **modem** via a telephone line. These offer a variety of services including downloading of **software**, communication with other users, **online database** (s) and online ordering. They may be run commercially or as a hobby, and telephone numbers are listed in some computer magazines.

bus A route around the computer consisting of a set of wires along which **signals** travel in parallel. These signals can start from any place on the bus and can travel to any destination. For example, in a **microcomputer** the **address bus** would carry signals to select a particular storage **location**; the **data** bus may then carry signals to transfer data to that location.

byte The minimum number of **bits**, usually enough to represent one **character**, that the computer can handle as one unit. The maximum number of bits it can handle as one unit is called a **word** and there may be several bytes in each word. As many computers use an eight-bit byte structure a byte is generally accepted to be 8-bits, a *nibble* being 4-bits and a *slice* 1-bit.

C

cache memory This is used to hold another copy of **data** which has recently been accessed by the **microprocessor** in anticipation of its use again in the near future. When next needed the data can be accessed very quickly, though the least accessed data in cache memory is replaced by newly accessed data.

calculator A machine which is able to do arithmetic (add, subtract, multiply and divide) and other logical operations. A programmable calculator is one which carries out a set of arithmetical operations in order according to a **program**. Even early calculators that worked with **punched cards** were able to follow simple programs, although they were not able to change their own programs or to do repeated **loops** and **branching**.

caps lock The facility on a **keyboard** which ensures that all letters pressed are sent to the computer as capital letters. Whereas the **shift** lock key affects all double entry keys, the caps lock only controls the letters of the alphabet. With the caps lock key on, some keyboards revert to lower case letters when the shift key is also pressed.

card punch A machine that punches holes in cards so that the cards store **data** which can be used at a later time. When **on line** the holes are punched by signals from the computer (300 cards per minute, say): **off line** they are punched by hand.

card reader A machine which reads cards

prepared by the **card punch**. The **data** stored on the cards is taken and put in another form (e.g. electrical **signals**) which can be used by a computer or other device. Reading speeds of over 1000 cards per minute are possible.

carry digit The **digit** that is carried over from one column to the next during addition. In denary adding 5+7 produces a sum of 2 with a carry digit of 1. In **binary notation** 1+1+0+1 produces a sum of 1 with a carry digit of 1.

cathode ray tube A normal television picture tube, as used in **monitors** and **visual display units**. Its advantage over a **liquid crystal display** at the present time is its superior brightness.

Ceefax The name of the BBC's **teletext** service which transmits data along with the normal programme transmissions. With a **teletext decoder** this **data** can be made to fill the **screen** (or be superimposed over the picture) one page at a time. Other broadcast data may be used by a computer's speech synthesizer to provide such things as talking newspapers. Commercial information is also distributed in this manner under the **Datacast** name, and could include **programs** and data for computers. This is one form of **telesoftware**.

central processing unit (CPU) The brains or nerve centre of a computer. It has three parts: its own **store**, an **arithmetic logic unit** and a **control unit**. The control unit carries out each instruction of a **program** in turn. This may involve arithmetic operations being carried out on **data** being held or the moving of data from one part of the computer to another. The central processing unit is sometimes known as the central processor.

Centronics interface This **parallel interface** is an accepted way of transferring **signals** between computer and **peripheral**, though is usually reserved for the **printer**.

character Any **keyboard** symbol. It can be a digit (0, 1, 2, ...), a letter (A, B, C, ...), a punctuation mark (!, ', ?, ...), a sign (*, +, −, ...) or just a space.

character code The **binary** code used by computers to represent **characters**. Each machine often has its own character code though there are some standard codes like **ASCII**.

character recognition Whereas computers can understand dots and punched holes, humans can read **characters**. To input characters into a computer one can use a **keyboard** to provide character codes though it would be much quicker if the computer could recognize written or printed characters. **Optical character readers** (OCR) and **magnetic ink** character recognition (MICR) are the two main systems of automatically recognizing characters.

chart recorder A record-keeping device that plots graphs by the movement of a pen to the right or left as a piece of paper is moved steadily in one direction underneath.

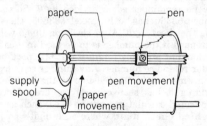

chart recorder

check digit An extra digit calculated from the original digits of a number and put on the end of that number. This is used to confirm that there has not been a change whilst data are being transferred either by hand or wire. This digit can be the result of a simple calculation, such as dividing by a predetermined number (a modulus); any remainder is then used to calculate the digit that has to be put at the end of the original number.

For example, to find the check digit for the number 63360 using modulus 7,

$$\frac{63360}{7}$$

gives a remainder of 3, indicating that thirty-something has to be exactly divisible by 7. With an extra digit 5 at the end, the new number will have no remainder when divided by 7. So the number 63360 has to be coded 633605, the 5 being the check digit. After checking this 5 will be dropped if the number is to be used in a calculation, but probably retained if it is a 'part' or similar reference number. Any number so coded will always be exactly divisible by the modulus providing it has been correctly entered. More complicated calculations can be used, such as a **weighted check digit**, where each digit's position in the number determines by how much it will be multiplied before being summed, divided and coded, thus reducing still further the chances of wrong entry.

checks on number tables, checks on strings
See **validation**.

checksum A meaningless total which is calculated by adding together a reference **digit** or number from each item in a file. Though meaningless in itself, the total should stay constant, and is used as a check that nothing has been lost when the **file** is transferred.

chip The common name for an **integrated ciruit**. It is a **solid state** circuit in which all the components are formed upon a single piece of **semiconductor** material. The first chip consisting of a **transistor** and a resistor was created in 1959. Since then the number of components on a chip has nearly doubled each year. LSI (**large-scale integration**) means an integrated circuit with more than 100 **logic gates** or over 1000 memory **bits**.

clock An electronic device that provides pulses at fixed time intervals. These pulses can be used to control the operations of a computer so that they are all in step (*synchronous*). Clock pulses are generated by an **astable** multivibrator.

coaxial cable A cable having two or more conducting wires each surrounding the one before though insulated from it (see overleaf). The outer conductor is usually 'earthed' so that the signals carried cannot be affected by external electric fields such as those generated by switching off other apparatus. Such cables are often used to connect a **microcomputer** to a television set or a **monitor**.

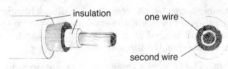

coaxial cable

COBOL (acronym for COmmon Business Oriented Language) A **high-level language** developed in America in 1959. It is most widely used for general commercial programming.

code 1. A set of programming instructions for a computer.
2. The binary patterns used to represent **characters**.

coded number A record number of an object. This can be made up, or coded, in a particular way to conform to a company or organization's particular computer system. Coded numbers can then be checked for validity by **check digit** or **weighted check digit** methods.

command Any word that is recognized by the computer as an instruction to do something. For example, **erase**, **list**, print, **run**. Note that some systems require commands to be in capital letters, whilst others demand a prefix (e.g. *, @, £) to denote how to interpret what follows.

communications (Comms) A technical word which covers the transfer of data from one place to another. In computer terms it is the connection between systems and includes, for example, Wide Area Networks (WAN), telephone lines, microwaves.

compact disc An **optical disc** of 4.75 inch diameter which can hold digital **data**. The size resulted from the requirement that it was to record up to 74 minutes of music, this being the duration of the longest classical works. New **programs** and data are 'burnt' onto the disc surface as dips by a strong laser. A weaker laser is able to read the surface by the reflected distortion from the dips as the disc rotates. Compact discs can incorporate programmed search and **memory** facilities and for music are regarded as giving perfect playback, no matter how many times they are used (no hiss and crackles, as with a conventional vinyl record). As the disc is rigid and no parts touch the surface, tracks can be densely packed together.

compact disc — Interactive (CD-I) A compact disc which digitally **stores** sound, picture, **text** and **software** but does not offer moving video. However it does offer a longer playing time of up to 20 hours if one drops the quality of the recording. Even at its worst, speech will be better than the normal radio broadcasts and by using a compression technique a single CD-I could hold in excess of 5000 still pictures. The user is able to *interact* with the disc by selecting what is to be retrieved.

compact disc — Digital Video Interactive (DVI) A compact disc which uses compression techniques to digitally store full-motion video pictures.

compact disc — Read Only Memory (CD-ROM) A compact disc used specifically as a **ROM** backing store for computers though requiring a special compact disk drive. CD-ROMs have a 550 mega**byte** capacity and are well suited for computer applications needing vast storage. For example, the whole of Europe's telephone directories could be stored on a couple of discs, and in fact the Post Office stores all Britain's 24 million postal addresses on one CD-ROM. The British Library is developing a complete catalogue of its books on a disc. The CD-ROM XA has extended architecture that includes audio and video.

compact disc — Photographic These discs are produced from photographic negatives or transparencies taken with a normal camera. To view the still-pictures the discs are placed in a Photo CD Player and as the data is held digitally it is possible to both enlarge and edit parts of the picture.

compatible Able to perform identically.

Although machines are made by different manufacturers compatible ones will work with the same **software** and **data interface** connections as each other.

compiler A **language**-translation **program** which converts instructions written in a **high-level language** into **machine code**. A compiler is different from an **interpreter** in that **instructions** (the **source program**) are entirely converted into **machine code** and saved (object program) before being **run**.

complement Because computers operate by 'adding' to existing **data**, then in order to subtract, binary arithmetic requires that negative value numbers be 'added' in the performance of subtraction.

For example,

$$\text{in denary} \qquad 13-6 = 7$$
$$\text{is the same as} \quad 13+(-6) = 7$$

To do this in binary requires
(a) A method of converting positive to negative (and viceversa), together with
(b) A 'bit' pattern' that can denote both positive and negative values.

Requirement (b) is achieved by assigning the left-most bit a negative value, whilst the conversion referred to in (a) is accomplished by finding the complement (or other part) of the bit pattern (one's complement) and adding 1 to it to give the two's complement (the true complement).

For example: using 6 bit binary,

Bit value	$-32+16+8+4+2+1$
	0 0 0 1 1 0
	is $-$ 0+ 0+0+4+2+0 = +6
One's complement	1 1 1 0 0 1
Add 1 to give	1
Two's complement	1 1 1 0 1 0
	is $-32+16+8+0+2+0 = -6$
and $13-6=7$	
would appear as	0 0 1 1 0 1
	$-$ 0+ 0+8+4+0+1 = +13
add -6 as above	1 1 1 0 1 0
	$-32+16+8+0+2+0 = -6$
to give	0 0 0 1 1 1
	$-$ 0+ 0+0+4+2+1 = +7

If the addition overflows to the left then this digit is ignored or dropped. From the above examples it will be seen that a quick check of the leftmost digit will indicate if the value shown is negative (1) or positive (0). See also **NOT gate**.

complex instruction set computer (CISC)
Computer architecture has been based on designing complex **microprocessors** so that eventually one **machine code** instruction is the result of translating one **high-level language** instruction. This means that microprocessors are

designed to use thousands of machine code instructions some of which are rarely used. In contrast, new **Reduced Instruction Set Computer** (RISC) microprocessors with simpler designs have higher speeds and can emulate and run existing **software** much faster.

computer An electronic **data-processing** machine that has three components where the input and **output** may be **digital** or **analogue** and the process would involve storage, control and arithmetical operations. A computer differs from most other machines because it is versatile and not restricted to doing one particular job. A **microcomputer** has a microprocessor as its **central processing unit**.

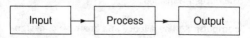

computer A block diagram of a computer's basic functions.

computer-assisted learning (CAL)
computer-based training (CBT)
computer-managed learning (CML)
These three entries refer to the use of the computer in education, the middle word in each case defining the use. Note the other variations listed

in the book and in the abbreviations section at the end. In the case of CAL the computer could display various pieces of information and ask particular questions depending on responses given by the user, thus assisting with the understanding of a topic. CBT uses the computer as a means of saying what the training course is, whereas with CML the computer not only provides the course but directs the student from one section to another according to progress and records the standards attained.

computer bureau   A company which sells time on its computer to many users. Thus a small firm can have the use of a large expensive computer quite cheaply, and in addition, have the help of the bureau if needed.

computing   The science and business of designing and applying information systems to solve problems and/or speed-up processes.

concatenation   The bringing together of sets of characters, usually as part of a program. For example, when a computer brings together the words 'GOOD', 'MORNING' and 'JACKIE' on its screen in response to Jackie switching on the machine and giving her **identifier** and **password**.

configuration All the pieces of **hardware** that make up the computer system. For example, a common micro configuration might consist of a microcomputer with 512 kilo**bytes** (1/2 megabyte) **random** access memory, a 3.5-inch **microfloppy disk** with 720 kilobytes capacity, a colour **monitor** and a **dot matrix** or **laser printer**.

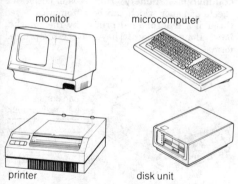

monitor

microcomputer

printer

disk unit

configuration The hardware in a computer system.

console This is what a computer operator uses; it may be a **visual display unit** plus a typewriter **keyboard**. This is called a **dumb**

terminal because it does not have any processing power of its own.

content addressable file store (CAFS) A system which allows rapid **data** selection or retrieval from **files** not by normal access through location **address** but by the file content.

continuous stationery   Hundreds of perforated sheets of paper which can be automatically fed through a **tractor-feed** printer by the sprocket holes along the sides. They may be pre-printed forms.

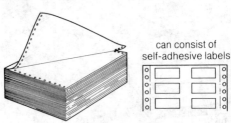

can consist of self-adhesive labels

continuous stationery

control character A character which when transmitted starts or controls a device. For example, a computer output having a particular character at the beginning may be routed to a printer, whereas with a different control character at the front it might be displayed on a **visual display unit**.

control register A **register** whose function is to hold the **address** of either the current **instruction** or the next instruction that the computer has to carry out. Also called the program counter.

control technology The use of computers and microelectronics to control external devices, often as part of automated systems.

control unit The part of the **central processing unit** which makes the computer carry out, in turn, each **instruction** of a **program**.

core store Before **solid state** memories this was the main type of store in all computers and consisted of rows and columns of small iron rings. They are like tiny washers which can be magnetized in one of two directions, clockwise, or anticlockwise, thus giving binary storage.

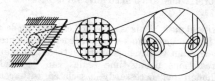

core store   Detail of construction.

counter Any device which continues to record 'the number of times' something is done. It might record the number of computer cards that are punched or, in the case of a **program**, the number of times a certain **loop** is carried out, though in the latter case the counter would be no more than a particular memory **location** whose value is increased by one each time. For example, in a program when the computer expects, say, a 6-**digit** number, a counter could be used so that it waits for six digits but will accept no more.

courseware The accompanying instructions that have to be followed together with the learning or training package **run** on the computer. Courseware may be printed so that it can be studied in the usual way but can be a part of the computer **software**.

Cray, Seymour (1925–) American designer of many of the most powerful computers in the world, which are named after him.

critical path This is a method of breaking down a large project into a series of ordered sequences. Each stage is then dependent on those before and predictions about time scales can be made. Though not necessarily associated with computers, the method of critical path analysis usually involves a large amount of calculation best done by a computer.

cross compiler A **compiler** used by one computer to produce a **machine code** program suitable for another, usually smaller, computer.

cursor Generally a rectangle the size of a capital letter which appears (sometimes flashing) on the **screen** of a **VDU** to indicate the current display position. Pressing a key should result in that **character** appearing on the screen in place of the cursor which is then displaced one character to the right.

cut and paste The facility, provided by some drawing **software** packages and **word processors**, where the user can mark an area of the **screen** (*cut*) and move it to another position on the screen (*paste*). Transfers to **memory** and to other files are also possible.

cybernetics The study of computer control in comparison with the human nervous system.

D

daisywheel printer This printer, as its name suggests, has a wheel with arms like the petals on a daisy. At the end of each arm there are two characters and these are pressed forward by a hammer to print on paper using a typewriter ribbon. It prints at a speed of about 50 characters per second and is generally noisy.

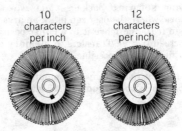

10 characters per inch

12 characters per inch

daisywheel printer

data A general term for numbers, digits, characters and symbols which are accepted, stored and processed by a computer. Only when such data becomes meaningful to a person can we say we have '**information**'. Thus terms such as 'information processing' and '**information retrieval**' are really '**data processing**' and 'data retrieval'.

database Files of structured **data** stored in a computer but arranged so that they can be accessed in many different ways for use in various applications. The idea is that the same data is stored only once but can be manipulated by the database management system so that data files can be shared by various pieces of **software**.

For example, a database might contain three files; one on names of firms, one on addresses and one on types of business. Access to all three files for a particular company might be made using the company's name or by using the company's address. Faster and more efficient retrieval can be achieved with a relational database. In this case links or relationships between items of data can be set up when the database is created, and this allows for easier retrieval by the user.

databus The route (set of wires) inside a computer along which the **data** travels to and from various locations. The **address** of the **location** is indicated by the **signals** which travel along the **address bus**.

data communications The process of transmitting **data** between equipment, often over long distances. Particularly in the past, computers and equipment were made to different standards by manufacturers, and it was not possible for direct communication between them. Thus, intermediary data packet systems are used which can change data into a form which can be communicated forward and then on exit, change the data into a form which can be used by the receiving computer.

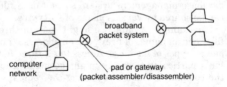

computer network

broadband packet system

pad or gateway (packet assembler/disassembler)

data communications How British Telecom transmits data in packets.

For example, British Telecom run a **Packet Switch Stream** (PSS) system using **Broadband**. On entry the data is assembled so it can use the system and is moved forwards in packets. At the required exit it is disassembled for use by the receiving computers. The Broadband system can forward voice, data, image and fax traffic.

The international telecommunications committee (CCITT) has recently approved a new communications standard which, if adopted, will make it possible for all computers and equipment to communicate over long-distance public systems. This is the X.400 standard. Existing CCITT standards include V.24 (RS232C) ports.

data compression A means of reducing the amount of **data** that has to be stored or transmitted.

For example when sending 0s and 1s, if there is a sequence of 350 consecutive 0s it is shorter to send 'repeat 0, 350 times' than to send the 350 0s one after the other. This method is often used with **archived files** and in **compact disc** storage.

datalogging A term used to describe the automatic collecting of **data** by a machine for a computer, the data being stored for later analysis. For example, a **microprocessor**-controlled central heating system repeatedly records data from the heat **sensors** in the different rooms around the building. This data would be kept and used to control the heating.

data processing (DP) The operation of collecting, storing, processing and transmitting **data**. A computer could be described as a data processing machine though a data processing system could involve clerical work and additional **hardware**.

Data Protection Act An Act of Parliament which came into force in May 1986. All organizations, businesses and institutions which hold computerized personal information on people have to register that fact. Individuals now have the legal right to view files held on themselves. There are some exceptions, such as police and medical records. A record containing wrong information can be ordered to be changed.

debugging A computer **program** may contain **errors** and these have to be found and corrected. As these errors are called **bugs**, correcting them is known as debugging. The three main types of error are logic errors (the program subtracts B from A instead of A from B); **syntax** errors (the instruction rules have not been properly used); and **run**-time or execution errors (such as drawing with the same foreground as background colour).

decimal An **integer** in the range 0 to 9 used in **denary notation**. Note that when working in denary (base 10) one uses the digits 0 to 1-less-than 10, that is 9. Similarly when working in a different base, say 6, one uses the digits 0 to 1-less-than 6, that is 5. In binary (base 2) we just use 0 and 1.

decision box A diamond-shaped symbol used in a **flowchart** to indicate a choice in direction. The choice usually depends upon the value of a **variable**.

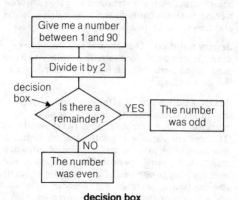

decision box

decoder This changes **data** from one coded form into another. For example, an instruction in a program such as PRINT would be stored in binary and as such would have to be decoded by **logic circuits** before it could be carried out. Also a decoder is used to change a **teletext** signal before it is displayed.

default   In order to speed up the decisions that can be made by the user, a **programmer** will often set the machine to '**allocate** the most likely instruction or value'. The user can therefore accept this default instruction or value without having to think through the possibilities, but is also free to make an alternative decision.

denary notation   Our normal system where we count in tens using decimals. The digits 0 to 9 are used in the units column before we carry over to the tens column.

desktop publishing (DTP)   A system of producing professional-quality reports, booklets and magazines on a computer and **peripherals**. A DTP system usually consists of a computer, a **mouse**, a laser **printer** and associated **software** (integrated **word processing**, graphics and page-making **programs**). More complex systems also contain a **scanner** for reproducing black-and-white photographs and other artwork.

   Text and graphics can be made up into magazine-type layout with a variety of **typefaces** and headings. Standard word-processing programs now incorporate many DTP features.

diagnostic routine   A program which may be supplied with the computer used for tracking **errors** in programs or for detecting faults within the machine. Useful for **debugging** programs.

digit Any of the figures 0 to 9, though note that the number 747 has three digits but only two different **characters**. To a computer a digit is part of an item of **data**.

digital Changing in discrete jumps and not continuously like **analogue** quantities.

For example, the time on a digital clock where the number changes by one each second. The two-state system used by digital computers only allows for discrete values to be stored, though these can be made more accurate by using more digits to record each value, e.g. the thousandths of a second shown by the digital time on the television **screen** at sports events.

digital computer This type of computer only works with data represented in a digital form, usually binary 0s and 1s. It differs from the analogue computer in that it can store large amounts of data and can calculate very accurately.

digitize The process of converting an **analogue** quantity to a **digital** one. For example, digitizing a picture by scanning involves dividing it into small areas (dots) and allocating values for brightness and colour which are then recorded as (digital) **data**.

digitizer A device which converts **analogue** signals into **digits**; that is, an A-to-D converter (analogue-to-digital). For example, in order that a computer might record readings of temperature one would connect the recording device to a computer via a digitizer. As the temperature rises so there would be a continuously increasing voltage input to the digitizer which is repeatedly scanned by the computer. The computer records the increases in finite jumps, storing the **data** as digits. Although the jumps can be made very small (thus giving greater accuracy and more significant figures) they always exist in the computer data.

direct-access storage Unlike **serial access memory**, direct-access storage can be reached very quickly and without any reference to previously accessed **locations**. Sometimes called **random access memory** (RAM), the **data** or **program** can be accessed almost instantly without having to go in sequence from the beginning because its **location** is known to the computer.

disk A flat circular plate covered in magnetic material which is able to store **data** on concentric tracks. As the disk spins a read/write head travels from edge to middle selecting only the required tracks. Each track is divided into **sectors**. A **format program** is used to lay down the tracks and sectors on a blank disk, and this has to be done on every new disk before it can be used. Disks allow fast direct **access time** compared to the much slower sequential access **tapes**.

disk operating system A **program**, often held in **read only memory** which controls the **disk** drive and the passing of **data** to and from the computer. Usually supplied by the manufacturer with a **microcomputer**.

disk unit A peripheral device consisting of a disk drive and one or more read/write units. Hard disks can be fixed in place (**Winchester Disk Drive**), or exchangeable, sometimes in sets of six. Removable ones for **microcomputers** are called **floppy disks**. When inside the unit the disks are accessed by the read/write head while they revolve at high speed.

documentation Printed information which usually accompanies a computer **program** and gives advice on how to use the package and what output can be expected. It may also include a **flowchart**, a program listing, a list of **variables** and testing procedures with sample **data**. Documentation is useful to the program user but is vital if modifications are to be made to the program.

document reader An input device for a computer whereby forms having marks in certain positions are read (can be at high speed) by a machine.

One example is a sheet of questions having multiple choice boxes

Age . . .   5 to 10   11 to 18   18 to 25   over 25
               ☐   ☐   ☐   ☐

to be completed by many people, their responses being quickly analysed by computer at a later time. Other examples include **marksense** cards, documents using **magnetic ink** (bank cheques etc.) and **optical character** recognition.

dot matrix printer A **printer** which forms characters on paper by printing a pattern of dots. The printing head consists of a set of needles mounted one above the other in a line. As the head moves sideways, certain wires are pushed forward to form a column of dots on the paper and several such columns form a **character**. Early matrix heads had seven needles, but were unable to print lowercase descenders (the tail of a g or y) until nine needles were introduced. There are now printers with 16, 18 and 24 needles. A range of colours can be achieved by using, say, a four-colour ribbon and overprinting in different colour(s).

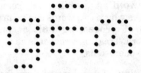

dot matrix printer   A nine-wire dot matrix printer uses five dots for a small letter plus two above for capitals and two below for lowercase descenders.

An improved imprint is obtained by printing each character twice, particularly if the second print is slightly out of line with the first, making the gaps between the dots less obvious. This is often called 'near letter quality' (NLQ).

Modern dot matrix printers can print up to 300 characters per second in draft mode and 60 characters per second in NLQ mode. They are preferred to **daisywheel printers** because they can print in a range of lettering styles and graphics and they are also quieter to operate. Although noisier and slower than **laser printers**, they have the advantage that because they are impact printers they can produce carbon copies of **hard copy**.

double buffering   The use of two stores or **buffers** in a computer where one can be analysed whilst the other is being filled and vice versa.

double word A facility of some **micro-computers** where two words can be processed by the **central processing unit** as one double-length word. Treating two words as a single unit speeds up operations.

downloading The taking of **data** from a large machine (**mainframe**) to a smaller one (**micro-computer**). This process might use the telephone, the radio or the television to provide the link between the two.

down time The length of time during which a machine is not usable due to faults of some kind.

dry run The term for using pen and paper to work through a program by constructing a **trace table** (a table showing the program pathway of variables and important events such as decisions). By inputting **data** and following the pathway and events, **run** time or execution errors can be spotted. Dry running a program is an important part of developing programs and saves time and costs later by reducing the number of **bugs**.

dumb terminal A **terminal** with no processing power of its own.

dump The process of copying the **data** in a section of **memory** and sending it to a **periph-**

eral device (a **printer**, say) or to a **backing store**.

duplex operation A mode of transmission which allows **data** to travel in both directions at the same time. It also displays on the **screen** the **character** typed as well as sending it to the computer. Half-duplex allows travel in both directions but not at the same time.

dynamic data exchange The ability to transfer **data** between different **applications packages** that are resident in a machine (for example, **spreadsheet** data to **word processing** data) even when one of the packages is not in use. Thus a word processed report that uses data from a spreadsheet is automatically updated when the spreadsheet figures are changed.

dynamic stop When running a **program** it may be necessary to draw the operator's attention to some factor or other. A dynamic stop jumps the program into an infinite **loop** at the same time indicating that something is wrong. Only after interaction by the operator will the machine resume processing.

E

echo The return to the screen of transmitted **data** so that it can be checked against the original to ensure that the transmission has been carried out correctly. **Keyboard** depressions are normally echoed to the **computer screen** for checking by the operator, as are **program** commands, but this is optional.

edge connector The protruding edge on a printed circuit board which carries the conduct-

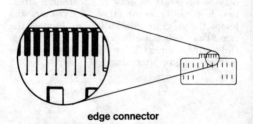

edge connector

ing paths so that they can join up with other devices. Most boards have several edge connectors allowing the board to be plugged into a socket.

edit The task of changing and improving a **program** by adding or removing instructions or by modifying the **data**. This is sometimes done with the help of a special program called an editor.

eight bit The word size of a computer, describing the maximum number of **bits** that it acts upon as a unit; similarly for 16-bit, 24-bit, etc. (though 8-bit has also been accepted as one **byte**).

electronic data interchange (EDI) The system of providing data relating to invoices, orders and other forms by exchanging tape or by using phone lines, electronic mail and computers. Purchasers and suppliers often have to complete many documents before business can be concluded, and in international trade customs points between countries make business slow, frustrating and full of delays to complete. At present, a project involving some of the biggest international motor and chemical companies is testing such an EDI system. Standards of interchange (OSI) have been agreed with the United Nations and the International Standards Organization (ISO). It is hoped that EDI will make the paperless transfer of documentation into a reality. See also **information systems**.

electronic funds transfer at point of sale (EFTPOS) A system of direct communication between a bank's computer centre and retail outlets (shops, garages, service points). A point of sale terminal is used to feed data directly to and from a customer's bank account. In this way an account can be debited instantly for any products purchased.

The point of sale terminal often has a **bar code** reader attached for reading bar-coded items (which communicates with automatic stock control/reordering systems) and a **magnetic strip** reader to provide data for the receiving computer. Prices and other transaction details could be obtained from EPROM chips within the terminal.

EFTPOS may herald the day of the cashless society, when we will rely on plastic cards and rarely use money.

electronic mail A system where **data** is sent from one place to another via a **telecommunications** link. A document created on a **word processor** could be changed or corrected and then sent via a satellite communications system from an office in one country to a **VDU** screen in another country. Here it could be held in

memory until required and then answered in the same way; no paper, no stamp, no postman; just an 'electronic office'.

electrostatic printer   This machine prints on paper by electrically charging selected areas of the paper (similar to rubbing a balloon on your sleeve and allowing it to hold itself on to the ceiling) so that they can attract a fine dust which is then permanently fused to the paper by heat.

emulator   A piece of **hardware** (though it can be **software**) which when attached to a computer makes it behave as if it was another type of computer. Thus **programs** prepared for one range of computers can, with the aid of an emulator, be run on another range of computers.

encoder   A device (such as a **keyboard** or position indicator on a turning shaft) which converts signals into the coded digital form required for the next process.

encryption   This is used for **security** and involves the changing of **data** so that it cannot be recognized let alone decoded except by an authorized receiver. It is carried out before the transmission of data and also used to hide **passwords** within computer **software**.

end mark   A code used when working with a

stream of **data** when it is necessary to indicate the end of various items.

ENTER key A key used to enter typed data. When a key is pressed on a computer **keyboard** the **character** is held in a **buffer** until the operator presses the ENTER key. At this point it becomes available to the **program** or operating system. This is also known as the RETURN key and may be labelled RET or marked with a bent backward arrow.

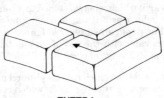

ENTER key

erasable storage A means of storage which can be used over and over again as new **data** overwrites the old data. Examples include magnetic **tapes** and magnetic **disks**.

erase The rubbing out of **data** that has been stored. However, unlike the rubbing out of a pencil line where nothing is left, in a computer it means replacing a code with another code that indicates 'the area of **memory** is now available for new data'. It might be zeros but this is not necessarily the case. Each time data is stored, whether it is in the computer's memory or on **disk** or **tape**, this new data overwrites or erases what was originally stored.

error   This is said to have happened whenever the results that are expected do not appear. Errors can be due to mistakes made in programming (**software** errors) or due to faulty equipment (**hardware** errors), or human operator mistakes.

error message   When an error occurs it may be possible for the **program** to indicate what has gone wrong by putting a message on the **screen**. Such wording is known as an error message and helps the user find the fault quickly.

For example, 'cannot divide by zero at line 230' is an error message which tells the operator that the value of the denominator is zero at instruction number 230 in the program.

escape key   The key on a computer **keyboard** that is used to interrupt a **program** while it is running. It can also be programmed to do other things such as restart the program.

exclusive-OR gate   A **logic gate** which operates with **binary digits**. Its **output** is of logic value 1 when any of its inputs have logic value 1 but not if all the inputs are 1. (**Inclusive-OR** also outputs a 1 if all the inputs are 1.)

For example, with a two input exclusive-OR the **truth table** shown below applies.

This gate could be used to sum two binary digits but does not give the carry digit.

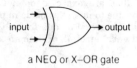

a NEQ or X–OR gate

Input		Output
0	0	0
0	1	1
1	0	1
1	1	0

exclusive-OR gate

execute   The carrying out of a **program** or of just a single instruction.

exit   The last instruction in a routine which would send the computer back to the main **program**; or it could be the ending of the whole program.

expansion port   The socket provided on a computer that allows the connection of additional circuit boards or equipment.

expert systems   A computer package that will enable the user to gain access to and use the knowledge and reasoning of experts. In the future these will operate so fast and have such large memories that using them will be like communicating with the expert.

F

facsimile   The scanning of a document and converting the shading into signals which can be transmitted via wires or radio waves. These signals are used to create a copy of the original document.

fail-safe   The system in a computer or **peripheral** device which allows it correctly to stop itself working should a fault occur.

fast line   Rates of transmitting **data** are usually given in **baud**. **Prestel** transmits to the user at 1200 baud but at greater speeds on the telephone lines data can get lost or muddled. Special direct lines, available from British Telecom, are able to transmit data at 48 000 or 96 000 baud and such lines are known as fast lines or data lines.

fault tolerant Having **backup** circuits so that should there be a failure then duplicates would automatically switch on. Sometimes a backup circuit repeats the activity of its main circuit so that no loss of **data** would occur during the switchover. Fault-tolerant computers are more expensive but deemed essential for applications where a computer failure would be almost disastrous, for example, in air traffic control.

feasibility study A study carried out before a company buys a new computer system. A team of experts would decide whether a computer was necessary and beneficial and if so which configuration of machines would best suit the company.

ferrite core A ring-shaped piece of magnetic material the size of a pinhead or smaller. Just as a bar or iron can be magnetized N-S or S-N so a ring can be magnetized clockwise or anticlockwise, and this is used for storing binary 0s and 1s. Such cores are built in rows to form what is known as the **core store** of a computer.

fibre optics A process using the transmission of light along a glass or Perspex® fibre. Light entering one end of a fibre is repeatedly reflected on the outside of the inner part until it reaches the other end. Total internal reflection takes place as two types of glass are used and this involves very little energy being lost at each reflection.

Such fibres are made very thin (less than 1 mm across) and are easily bent. Thus a cable consisting of many fibres can be laid in just the same way as normal copper ones. Up to 32 000 simultaneous telephone conversations can be carried for the same size of cable. Normal electrical signals (carrying data) are used to modulate a laser light beam which is sent to a receiver along an optical fibre.

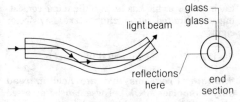

fibre optics

field In a **database**, each **record** is broken down into fields. In a personnel system, one field might hold 'names', another the corresponding 'dates of birth'. Searches can be carried out on the different fields.

For example, find all persons named BROWN and born between 1966 and 1970.

fifth generation computers Advanced and powerful computers which will appear during the 1990s and offer **expert systems**, many **program** languages and **parallel processing**. Thirty or more times faster than the best **fourth generation computers**, they will offer speeds of 1 billion instructions per second (1000 mips).

file Just as sheets of paper form a file in a filing cabinet so a collection of **data** can form a file suitable for use by a computer. The file can be in **backing store** or in the computer's **memory**. Each computer file has its own file name consisting of a limited set of **characters**, say six or eight.

file inversion See **inverted file**, **sort**.

firmware Programs that are held in **read only memories** (ROM). These can be accessed very quickly and are not lost when the machine is switched off (non-**volatile** memory). Thus they do not have to be loaded into the computer as they are permanently available in the machine.

first generation computers   These computers, built in the 1940s and early 50s, used electronic valves, whereas the **second generation**, built between the mid-50s and the mid-60s, used transistors. The **third generation** used **integrated circuits**.

fixed-point arithmetic   This system involves having the decimal point of every number in the correct place, though the position can be set before a calculation (i.e. all figures to two decimal places). This does limit the size of numbers though it permits faster calculations by the computer. See also **floating-point arithmetic**.

flag   An indicator added to the end of a piece of **data** which might be used to indicate an error or to make the **hardware** perform a **branch** to another part of the **program**.

flip-flop   A basic electronic circuit which remains in one of two possible states until it receives a **signal**. It then switches over to the other state and waits for the next signal before switching back. Known technically as a **bistable** multivibrator it can be used as a storage device (two states: one for 0 and one for 1) or for division by two as two input pulses are required to get it to give out one pulse.

floating-point arithmetic   Unlike **fixed-point**

arithmetic, these numbers are recorded as a set of digits together with the power to which their base is raised. For example, the denary number 789.249 would be stored as (+0789249) and (+3). Most scientific **calculators** use this method which, although slower in calculations, gives a very much wider range of numbers. Note the convention of using E so that the number can be written as 0.789249E3 and that the EE key converts this to 7.89249E2.

floppy disk A flexible magnetic disk used for supplying and storing **data** for a **microcomputer**. When the disk rotates inside its cardboard jacket (say 300 r.p.m.) in a **disk unit** it

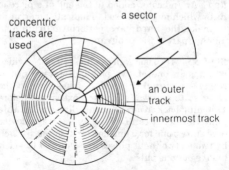

floppy disk   A mini-floppy disk.

becomes rigid and can be 'read' by the read/write head. The area used for recording is a band of concentric tracks each of which is divided into **sectors**. Disks may be single or double sided, double or high density and **soft** or **hard sectored**. They are generally available in three sizes: 3.5-inch (microfloppy), 5.25-inch and 8-inch diameters. Developments in technology mean that the latest 3.5-inch **microfloppy** high density disks can store up to 1.4 mega**bytes** (this is achieved by aligning the magnetic dipoles vertically instead of horizontally to the disk's surface).

flowchart A set of special boxes or shapes drawn on paper and connected by lines to show the order of a set of events. They are used by **programmers** to describe the sequence of operations to be carried out by a computer (see overleaf).

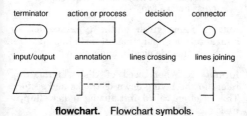

flowchart. Flowchart symbols.

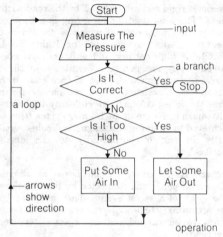

flowchart The flowchart for adjusting the pressure of a tyre.

font A name given to the **typeface** for all **characters** and punctuation including the size. Examples include pica 10 and roman 8.

format 1. When used of **disks**, formatting refers to the laying down of tracks and sectors. This is often called initializing a new **floppy disk**.

2. In **word processing**, formatting means arranging the layout of a piece of **text** in a particular way before it is printed.

fourth generation computer These are the computers built during the 1980s with capacities of 5000 K and speeds of 30 million instructions per second (30 mips).

fourth generation languages (4GL) These are the most recent types of programming languages, each being designed for a particular type of application. By using predefined **screens** and natural **text**, they assist **programmers** and non-experts alike, to describe their application. The **code** generation can be almost automated after this stage thus enabling time and cost to be greatly reduced.

frame   1. An often misunderstood word in that it describes one screenful (about 150 words if all **text**) of **information** on the **Prestel** system. Prestel pages can consist of one or more frames.
  2. It is also used to describe one row of holes across a **paper tape** (which is the code for a single character) and one bit of store across a magnetic **tape** (a 0 or 1).

friction feed The method of feeding paper through a **printer** whereby the paper is held by friction between rollers. For long runs of printing which require accuracy **tractor feed** would be used.

full-adder A logic circuit (which consists of a set of **gates**) which has three inputs and two outputs. It is used to add together two **binary digits** and the **carry digit** from the previous column giving both the sum and the next carry digit.

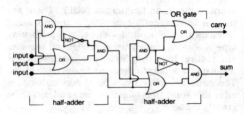

full-adder A full-adder circuit comprising two half-adders.

function code One of a computer instruction's two parts. The function, or **operation code** states what has to be done (add, subtract, print) and the other part indicates on what (numbers, **address**).

function keys The additional keys on a computer **keyboard** that are programmed by the manufacturer or can be programmed by the user so as to enter a specific **code**. They are often used as an alternative to having to press two or more keys thus saving time (and error) for the user. Such keys can be used to store both a **command** and also a complete procedure or a **subroutine**.

fuzzy logic Whereas **boolean algebra** uses TRUE and FALSE logic, here there is also a third alternative, MAYBE. Each of the various options are allocated a percentage factor and the route then taken will not always be the same. Used in conjunction with **heuristic programs** and in modelling situations such as 'war games'.

G

gallium arsenide A **semiconductor** that is used instead of silicon when high speed circuits are required on a **chip**. The other advantage is that they require less power though they are at present much more expensive to make.

garbage The name given to meaningless **data**. Such rubbish is printed by a computer because of errors in the program or in the data or because the data belongs to another **program**. 'Garbage in–Garbage out' (GIGO) is a well known saying with regard to computers.

gate Electronically, this word refers to a part of a **transistor** although it is generally used to describe a **logic circuit** with several inputs and one or two **outputs**. An **AND gate** is an example where the output depends on the logic state of the inputs. Such gates form the basic building units of all calculating **chips**.

gateway The facility in communications of being able to access other computer services from within the **on-line** service being used.

gigabyte (GByte) Originally the term for 1024 **megabytes** (MB or MByte) but increasingly being used to mean 1000 megabytes (1 000 000 000 **bytes**).

graphical display A unit, rather like the **screen** of a television set, which is used to display both **text** and drawings. Sometimes a **light pen** can be used by the operator to get the **computer** to make changes to the display.

graphical user interface The facility that enables the user to work with **icons**, and a **mouse** rather than **text** (i.e. rather than selecting A, B or C from a **menu**). Sometimes referred to as a **WIMP environment**, it aims at presenting the user with a familiar screen display and a consistent operating procedure for all the **programs** likely to be resident (and probably integrated) in the machine. It also offers use of the **operating system**, together with various enhancements, whilst still maintaining the familiar appearance.

graphics tablet   An input device that, by sensing pressure, translates the position of a pen or pointer on a pad into a digital **signal** for a computer. It enables the user to draw or trace a shape to the computer **screen** and into **memory**. It can also be used to amend existing digital pictures which may have been taken from a painting, photograph or video-still.

H

half-adder   A **logic circuit** (which consists of a set of **gates**) which has two inputs and two **outputs** (see overleaf). It is used to add together two **binary digits** giving both the sum and the **carry digit**. See **full-adder**.

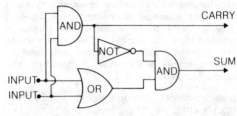

half-adder

handshake Signals such as 'ready to receive', 'transmit', 'acknowledge', 'wait', which help to control **data** transfer between **computers** and **peripherals**. It is similar to humans saying 'Hello, can you spare a minute?'.

hardcopy The printed **output**, usually on paper, which can be taken away and studied.

hard disk store A disk sealed into its unit. As the disk is not removable, the read/write head is extremely close to its surface and tracks can be densely packed together. Because of precision engineering, a hard disk has far greater capacity than a floppy disk, typically up to 140 mega**bytes** for micro equipment. As with floppies, **data** and **programs** can be added, revised and removed with **software** commands. Hard disks are also known as **Winchester disk drives**.

hard sectored   This describes the way in which the length of a **sector** on a **floppy disk** is set. In this case small holes (say 6 or 12 in a ring) near the centre hole of the disk fix the position of each sector: as the disk revolves they indicate the change from one to the next.

hardware   All the equipment that makes up the **computer** system. If it can be picked up and carried then it is hardware as opposed to **software**.

hardwired logic   The logic that is built in to an **integrated circuit** (or **chip**) by the manufacturer and refers to the wiring between **gates** as well as the gates themselves.

hash total   Sometimes called a *batch total*, this is the result when the computer adds together a reference **digit** or number from each item in a file, thus giving a meaningless or hash total. It is used on future occasions to check that all the items have been accessed.

hertz   The standard unit of frequency. The basic unit (Hz) is one cycle per second so in the fast speeds of computing kilohertz (KHz, that is 1000 hertz) and megahertz (MHz), one million hertz, are used. Named after the German physicist Heinrich   Rudolph   Hertz   (1857–94),   the first person to produce electromagnetic waves artificially.

heuristic program A **program** so written that each time it runs it learns from the results of its own actions and makes changes to improve its performance the next time.

hexadecimal notation In this system one counts in 'sixteens' instead of 'tens'. Usually the digits 0 to 9 are used and the letters A, B, C, D, E and F represent ten, eleven, twelve, thirteen, fourteen and fifteen. Whereas in a four-digit number in **denary** each digit in turn represents thousands, hundreds, tens and units, in HEX each digit would represent 4096s, 256s, 16s and units.

Thus

$$A60B = (10 \times 4096) + (6 \times 256) + (0 \times 16) + (11 \times 1)$$

$$= 42\,507 \text{ in denary}$$

The reason why HEX is used by **computers** is because of the way numbers are stored. To store the numbers 0 to 9 in binary, four digits are required, 0000 to 0101. Thus for our normal numbers we have to use four **binary digits**, but with four binary digits we can store not just 0 to 9, but 0 to 15. That is 0000 to 1111. So by working in sixteens we can use all the available storage codes that the computer can offer.

high-level language A **programming language** in which instructions are written in normal or everyday language, but in a rigidly prescribed manner (**syntax**). This enables the **programmer** to write, read and understand them more easily than **machine code** into which each instruction must be converted before a **computer** can follow them. Each high-level instruction may convert into several machine code instructions; this can be done in a number of ways:

(a) One instruction at a time whilst the **program** is running, using an **interpreter**. In this case the computer is always waiting for the interpreter to do its job, and this happens every time the program is **run**, hence it slows operation.

(b) The program can be entirely converted into machine code and saved before it is run, using a **compiler**. This compiled program in machine code is then available for immediate use whenever required.

Each high-level language has been designed for optimum performance in certain circumstances. For example, **BASIC** for beginners, **COBOL** for business and commercial applications, **ALGOL** and **FORTRAN** for mathematical and scientific use.

high resolution graphics Most microcomputers offer some form of graphics whereby the

programmer is able to plot points and draw lines. The graphics **screen** is divided into an 'X' horizontal axis and a 'Y' vertical axis. The whole area is composed of **pixels** (picture elements). As a rough guide, 640 by 480 pixels is considered high resolution, whereas 320 by 240 would be low resolution.

Special graphics **dumps** are required to read the screen and send the pixel data to a **printer** or **plotter**.

high resolution graphics

Hollerith, Herman (1860–1929) American inventor who realized that the results of the 1890 United States census could not be worked out by hand before the 1900 census was due and so devised a card-reading machine to analyse the census details. **The punched card** code he invented allowed all twenty-six letters and the numbers 0 to 9 to be coded in twelve punching positions. Known as the Hollerith Code, it is still in use today.

hopper A device that holds punched cards ready for feeding to a **card punch** or **card reader**.

housekeeping Routines, sometimes within a **program**, that are carried out when time is not of importance. For example, the setting up of suitable **fields** or entry conditions or the allocation of areas of **store** or the updating of the master record-keeping **file**.

I

icon A small pictorial symbol on the **screen** which can be activated by the **cursor** or a **mouse** in order to instruct the **computer** to do a particular task like load or display a **data** chart, or run a particular program to save the user having to type in a series of **commands**.

identifier A name or set of **characters** chosen by the **programmer** which indicates which **file** or which **store** is to be used at that point in the **program**.

image-processing The processing of digital **data** that represents a picture which may have been a painting, photograph, satellite image or video picture. The user is able to change selected parts of the picture at will (e.g. a particular shade of red, the shape of an object).

immediate access store This is used to describe those **memories** where **data** can be accessed in times of one millionth of a second (a microsecond) or less. Included would be those stores within the **central processor** and those directly addressable by the **programmer**.

inclusive-OR gate A **logic gate** which operates with **binary digits**. Its output is of logic value 1 when any of its inputs has a logic value 1 otherwise it is 0.

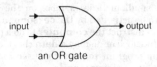

an OR gate

Input		Output
0	0	0
0	1	1
1	0	1
1	1	1

inclusive-OR gate The truth table applying to a two-input inclusive-OR gate.

indexed sequential access The storing and retrieving of **data** from a sequence of stores whose **addresses** have to be first found by the **computer** from an index **file**.

indirect address See **address**.

informatics The international term for microelectronics and **information** processing; it may be studied, applied or practised.

information Knowledge obtained from **data** by humans when they apply a set of rules. For example, the data on this page is conveying information to the reader (the author hopes) because a set of rules (i.e. English words and sentences) are being applied by the reader. Note that a **computer** really only deals with data.

information handling The ability to collect, create, store, retrieve, change, interpret, validate and present information.

information retrieval Obtaining information from **data** often stored in a **database**. In the past 'finding out' took time, allowing the user to think and plan. With today's **on-line databases** one has to plan the search route before starting, as pages of **information** appear so quickly.

information systems All those pieces of equipment which manipulate **data** (create, **store**, **sort**, transmit, display) and provide us with **information**.

information technology The acquisition, processing and distribution of information by microelectronics systems through computers and telecommunications.

initialize The setting up of the values of the **variables** at the start of a **program** so as to clear the values set by the previous run. For example, **counters** would be set to zero or their initial values.

ink-jet printer A printer in which a fine jet of quick-drying ink is fired at the paper forming **characters** as it lands. The ink droplets become charged as they are fired through the jet (or jets) and can then be bent into shape by a varying electric field. Speeds as high as 200 characters per second can be achieved and the device has the advantage of not being limited by the number of metal characters that can be positioned for printing. In addition character sets and type styles can be controlled by the **program** and many different languages can be printed with the same printer.

input buffer A section of **memory** reserved for

temporary storage of input **data** until the machine is ready to process it. For example, it is used whilst typing takes place on the **keyboard** so that alterations, additions and deletions can be made prior to the pressing of the **ENTER key**. Also used by **printers** to hold the **text** that follows whilst printing.

input device The device with which the operator enters both programs and data into a computer. Examples include **punched cards** or **punched tape**; also **light pens**, **keyboards**, **bar code readers** and **optical** or **mark sense readers**.

instruction The part of a **computer program** which tells the computer what it should be doing at that stage. For example, print or add.

instruction address register (IAR) This stores in turn the **addresses** of the instructions that the computer has to carry out. If during the running of a **program** you could look inside this **register** you would find that it contained the address of the next instruction to be carried out.

insulator A material that has a very high resistance to electric current so that the current flow through it is negligible. One of the best insulators known is silicon dioxide which is created on the surface of **silicon** by heating.

integrated circuit A **solid state** circuit in which all the components are formed upon a single piece of **semiconductor** material. The first one consisted of a **transistor** and a resistor and was created in 1959. Since then the number of components on a '**chip**' has nearly doubled each year. LSI (**large scale integration**) means an integrated circuit with more than 100 **logic gates** or over 1000 memory **bits**.

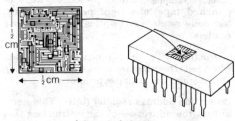

$\frac{1}{2}$ cm

←— $\frac{1}{2}$ cm —→

integrated circuit

integrated services digital network (ISDN) A telephone network depending on **fibre optics** and microwave links to carry computer-controlled **digitized** messaging **signals** originating from a variety of sources and equipment. Such signals can transmit voice, video, computer **data**, **electronic mail** and fax, separately or simultaneously. The only limitations are the different operating methods and protocols in use locally by companies and/or countries, with the ultimate aim being the possibility of sending all types of message, however generated, from anywhere to anywhere else in the world, speedily and without complications.

The phone network exists, and the digitizing and transmission of a variety of messaging forms controlled by computer is already taking place. All that remains is to integrate all these services on a world-wide basis.

integration The running on a computer system of several different **software** packages at the same time (e.g. **word processor**, **spreadsheet** and graphics) with the facility for the user to transfer **data** from one package to another.

intelligent terminal A **terminal** which retains a **program** and allows processing of **data** to be carried out without further access to the host computer.

interface This is the circuitry (or **hardware**) needed between two devices so that they can be connected together. Such a circuit board might compensate for differences in speed-of-working or transmission speeds or might translate the **codes**. Often it is the type of transmission that has to be changed and the interface is attached inside one of the devices.

interpreter A type of **program** which checks, translates and carries out a written program one statement at a time. Most home **micro-computers** use a Basic interpreter when running a BASIC program written by the user. Though satisfactory for most purposes this is much slower running that a Basic **compiler**.

interrogate The action by the user in constructing a query so as to search selectively for **information** from a **database** package.

interrupt A system whereby a peripheral device can stop the computer in its current task and use it to transfer **data** to or from that **peripheral**. The computer would then return to continue its work.

inversion The process of changing something into its opposite. Inversion of binary number 101 would produce 010 as each **binary digit** is changed to the opposite one. Using inversion and adding +1 to the result enables us to find the two's **complement** of a binary number.

inverse video The result when the computer reverses the colour and background on a **mono-chrome screen**. For example, instead of white **characters** on a black screen we get black characters on a white screen.

inverted file   A method of organizing a **file** so that groups are identified by 'keys'. Thus retrieving various groups is much quicker than by the normal method of searching every record. As **information retrieval** becomes widely used so file inversion becomes more important.

iteration   A mathematical process by which one obtains an answer and then uses that answer to obtain a more accurate one. The new answer is then used to obtain an even better one and so on. Whereas with pencil and paper such a method would be long and slow, with a computer it is a very useful way of finding the best answer correct to a significant number of places.

J   K

Jacquard, Joseph   (1752–1834) French inventor who developed the technique of using punched cards to store machine operating instructions. His automatic weaving loom was controlled by the punched holes in cards.

job The term used to cover all the activities involved in completing any project on a computer from start to finish. A job usually has many processes and can require several **programs**.

job control language A set of **commands** designed for a particular computer which are used to run a **program**. Such commands may involve loading a **compiler**, reading in the program, allocating **memory** and processing time and managing the **printer output**. The same set of commands may be used regularly and in such case would be stored as a job control **file**.

Josephson memory The ultimate magnetic **memory** device which will operate at up to a hundred times faster than today's best **chips** with even greater reductions in power consumption. These memory cells are kept at very low temperatures using a liquid gas. With several problems still to be solved Josephson memories are not likely to be readily available until the late 1990s.

joy stick An **input device** for a **microcomputer**. The stick as it moves (usually in one of eight directions) is able to control the movement of a shape on the **screen**. It does this by working two potentiometers (like a volume control on a radio), one recording its movement in the X-direction and the other in the Y-direction.

Sometimes there are two joy sticks enabling a screen game to be played by two players. A similar device, the **mouse**, is used with business **programs** and **WIMP environments**.

justify The adjustment of the positions of words so that the left-hand or right-hand margins or both, are regular. This is easily done on **text** by a computer before it is printed.

For example, the paragraph above is both left and right-hand justified whilst this paragraph is only left-hand justified, the lines being different lengths.

keyboard A device for coding **characters** onto **punched cards**, punched **tape** or directly into a computer which may or may not display them on a **screen**. In addition to the standard typewriter (**QWERTY**) pattern there are numeric keys, user definable keys, **hexadecimal** keys and others.

keyword Often used in **information retrieval** systems whereby items containing the given keyword are accessed by the computer and retrieved. In simpler systems only the titles of the stored items may be searched for the particular keyword though with some **main frame** computers every word in the **database** can be checked.

kilobyte A measure of storage capacity and equal to 1024 **bytes** (=1 K). An 8-**bit** computer with a capacity of 32 K locations would have 32 768 bytes or 32 kilobytes (each location holds one word and in this case 1 word=1 byte). A 16-bit computer with 512 K words of main memory might have two bytes in each word and thus a capacity of 1 048 576 bytes or 1048 kilobytes.

kimball tag A small piece of card with holes, usually attached to goods in a shop and removed at the time of purchase. These are used as **punched card** input for a computer which is thereby able to keep sales records and provide management reports. Instead of holes the **data** is sometimes coded in a magnetic strip on the tag.

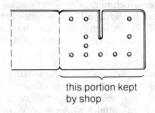

this portion kept
by shop

kimball tag

L

language In order to tell a computer what to do we have to use a language it understands. In addition the language we use must be precise with no chance of a double meaning. Such languages have been developed over the years from **machine code** and **mnemonics** to **high-level languages** like **BASIC** and **PASCAL**.

For example, it is clear why we cannot use ordinary English if one considers the words *PITCH* and *FAST* and all the different meanings that they have. There are at least five for each in everyday use, as listed on page 248 at the end of this book.

large scale integration (LSI) A measure of the number of **logic gates** on a **chip** about half a centimetre square. **Small scale integration** (SSI) about 1961, has less than 20; **medium scale integration** (MSI) about 1965, between 20 and 100; and large scale integration about 1969, above 100. Today we have VLSI (above 5000) and VVLSI though the **acronym** LSI is the one that is commonly used.

Note that the **microprocessor** is a special LSI

chip and that the LSI chips used in watches and **calculators** are unlikely to be microprocessors. Current practice is to produce an **uncommitted logic array** (ULA) chip which can have its logic gates connected in different ways for different customers. This is a cheaper and quicker way of obtaining a special type of chip as only one stage of manufacture is particular to that customer. However, the design is limited by the original logic gates and the possible connections between them.

lasercard Invented in California, this is a form of plastic card, the same size as a bank or credit card, with a silver surface on the back. Up to 2 mega**bytes** of **data** can be 'burnt' as dips in the surface. The lasercard can then be read by a weak laser. Data such as bank account details, medical history, digitized pictures, fingerprints, signatures or X-rays can be stored on one card.

Updating is possible in a similar manner to **compact disc-interactive** (WORM technique): a strong laser is used to burn new data onto unused parts of the card, with the added benefit of leaving an **audit trail** as an extra protection against misuse. Given its large storage, its security benefits and cheapness of manufacture, the lasercard is expected to be widely used across many applications in the future, much as the common credit card is today. Research is at present being conducted into lasercards with 10 megabytes capacity.

laser printer   This non-impact **printer**, which prints a page at a time, uses a dry copying process. The image is projected onto a light sensitive plate using a laser beam and the plate is covered with powder which is then transferred to paper. Such printers are capable of speeds of 10 pages per minute, high resolution graphics, and are beginning to offer good colour but are expensive. It is sometimes referred to as a *xerographic printer*.

least significant character   In a set or row of **characters** the one in the furthest right-hand position is the least significant one.

left justification   1. The arranging of lines of **text** so that the left-hand edges are all in line. 2. **Data** stored in consecutive **locations** all of which have been filled from the left though may have a different number of spaces on the right (similar to **right justification**).

library software   The **programs** and **routines** available to all the computer users. They form part of the facilities of the computer.

light emitting diode (LED)   A small coloured device that emits light like a bulb. It is particularly useful as an indicator lamp in such things as computers, television sets and radios as it requires a very low current and works at low voltages. Used in the past in **calculators** and **digital** wrist-watches, it has been largely replaced by **liquid crystal displays** (LCD) which consume even less power.

light guide Glass or perspex fibre used to transfer optical signals. Light enters at one end and is totally internally reflected along the **fibre optic**, i.e., guided by the fibre.

light pen Used with a **graphical display** unit the light pen allows the operator to draw, change and move sections of the picture simply by moving it across the **screen**. The pen is connected by

light pen

cable to the computer and the operator uses keys to control the changes. A **cathode ray tube** picture is produced by a dot which moves across the screen in lines (normally 625) and the position of the pen on the screen is worked out by the computer from the timings of the dot as it passes. Although the original programming for a light pen is complicated its use can enable designs to be created and changed very quickly. For example, certain shades can be stored in the computer's memory and then created on the screen in positions set by the pen just by pressing a key.

line feed This is a movement caused by an instruction in a **program** or a button on a **printer**, where the **screen** display or the paper in the printer moves to the next line. In the first case the display moves up a line; in the other the paper moves.

line number A number that tells the computer that what follows is part of a **program**. It is used in **BASIC** to show the order in which **instructions** are to be carried out, although some instructions may **branch** to self-contained **functions** or **procedures** located elsewhere in the program.

line printer A cylinder which has rows of **characters**. The As are in one row, the Bs in the next row, and so on. When a line is to be printed

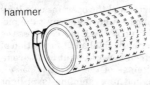

hammer

paper between hammers and drum

line printer

the cylinder turns so that all the As are printed, then turns so that all the Bs are printed, then the Cs; the whole line being printed in one revolution of the cylinder. Printing speed is between 500 and 3000 lines per minute but the lines printed are usually wavy.

The line printer would print 'COLLINS COMPUTER GEM' on one line by printing like this:

```
C          C
C          C          E   E
C          C          E   GE
C   I      C          E   GE
C  LLI     C          E   GE
C  LLI     C  M       E   GEM
C  LLIN    C  M       E   GEM
COLLIN     COM        E   GEM
COLLIN     COMP       E   GEM
COLLIN     COMP       ER  GEM
COLLINS    COMP       ER  GEM
COLLINS    COMP       TER GEM
COLLINS    COMPUTER   GEM
```

liquid crystal display (LCD) A liquid whose molecules can be made to line-up thus making it look darker when an electrical voltage is applied. They are used in seven-**segment displays** displays on watches and **calculators** as they require little power. Some liquid crystals change in colour with temperature and can be used as crude thermometers.

list Generally referred to as the listing on **screen** or paper of the **program** statements in number order. To follow the program statements in execution order one would use a **trace** facility.

load The reading of **program** statements or **data** from **backing store** into the appropriate parts of the computer **memory**.

location The places in a computer that are able to store **data**. Each location is identified and accessed by its **address** and the number of **characters** that can be stored in a location depends upon the particular machine.

local area network (LAN) The connecting together of several microcomputers for the fast exchange of **data** and the sharing of **peripherals** like **printers** and **modems**. Various configurations are available such as ring, star, bus and tree (see overleaf).

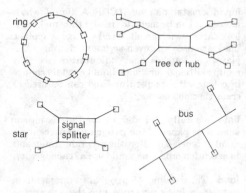

ring

tree or hub

star

signal
splitter

bus

local area network Four different LAN
configurations.

logic circuit The basic building blocks of
digital electronics often referred to as a **gate**.
AND, **OR**, **NAND** and **NOR** are all examples of
logic circuits and it is these that make up the
circuits on a **silicon chip**. In an **uncommitted
logic array (ULA)** chip sets of logic circuits
await interconnection to achieve the required
circuit pattern.

log in/on/off/out The terms used when entering or leaving a large computer system from a

terminal. In this way the number of users can be limited and the type of use restricted.

LOGO A powerful **high-level language** designed in 1969 by Seymour Papert. Developed to allow the exploration of ideas by both young and old, it offers experience in how to use a computer. Its strengths include **turtle** graphics (building shapes and patterns by moving a **screen** marker), list processing, **procedures** and **database** management. Logo can also be used on control tasks with floor turtles and other microelectronic devices. It is widely used in education.

look-up table A facility which allows one set of numbers or values to be directly related to another set. The dialling-codes of all the towns and cities in the United Kingdom could be stored in a **table** in the **memory** of a computer. If we type in the place name, say Cambridge, the computer would use a 'look up table' to find the correct dialling-code, which would be 0223 in this case. Such a table would be arranged as an **array**. It is used in a **spreadsheet** and many other commercial **programs**.

For example, an invoicing program would refer to a **database** for details of all goods or services, all of which would be liable to certain tax rates according to which group they were in. To avoid the large amount of work required when tax rates are changed, instead of each item having its individual tax level recorded for use in calculations, it is given a certain position in a table. This table carries the values to be given to each position.

Position	0	1	2	3	4	5	6	7	8
Tax rate %	0	5	10	12.5	15	17.5	20	25	30

So, if many items were taxed at certain levels and then the tax was increased by one point, all that needs to be done is to alter the look-up table and everything is immediately ready for use.

Similar methods can be used to decide quantity discounts on invoices, where the principle of 'the more you buy the bigger the discount' applies. Quantities supplied would be added up, and the computer program would use the look-up table to determine the appropriate discount.

Quantity bought	50	100	200	500	items
Percent discount	2	3	3.5	3.75	

loop Just as a loop of thread comes back to where it started so does a loop in a computer **program**. One difference is that the program continues to loop back UNTIL a certain condition is satisfied.

For example, the sorting of a set of numbers into ascending order would involve the computer in carrying out a sequence of instructions over and over again (a loop) UNTIL all the numbers were sorted. One way is to:

COMPARE THE FIRST AND SECOND NUMBERS
IF FIRST IS GREATER, INTERCHANGE NUMBERS
NOW REPEAT THIS LOOP WITH 2nd & 3rd NOS and so on
REPEAT LOOP when all the numbers have been dealt with, starting with first and second numbers again,
UNTIL a run through of all the numbers without any changes means that they are in order.

Note that a loop inside another loop is called a nested loop.

low-level language A computer **language** which is similar to, and therefore easily converted into, machine **code**. Each **instruction** is converted into one machine code instruction that is executed by the computer as a single operation. Programming using these languages is difficult as they depend on the type of **central processing unit** used and are not portable across different computers. They are used when operating speed is of importance, and 6502, Zilog X80 and Intel 80286 assembly are some examples of popular low-level languages. With a **high-level language** (such as **BASIC** or **FORTRAN**) one instruction would involve many machine code operations on the part of the computer, but programming is easier.

low resolution Where the eye can detect the limitation of a **cathode ray tube** screen and diagonal lines are clearly made up of steps. Usually occurs when there are fewer than 300 **pixels** across the **screen** width.

M

machine code The coding that makes the computer carry out its various tasks. The types of **instruction** and the way they have to be written are specified by the computer manufacturer. Machine code programming has often to be done in **binary notation** and is used when fast operation is required.

For example, Instruction number 634 might be to subtract (code 2) the contents of **location** 102 from the contents of 101 and put the answer in location 103. This might be machine coded as

| 634 | 2 | 101 | 102 | 103 |

It should be clear that programming in machine code is slow and tedious. The **programmer** has to keep track of what is held in each location and specify these locations in each instruction. To make things easier manufacturers supply an assembly language or **assembler** which uses words and letters to represent operations and **addresses**.

SUB A, B, C

would mean subtract the value of B from the value of A and let C be the value of the answer. The assembler translates each instruction into one machine code instruction. For easier programming a **high level language** such as **BASIC** is used and the instruction becomes

LET C=A−B   or even
C=A−B   as LET is optional

A **compiler** or **interpreter** would then be used to translate such an instruction into machine code, though many machine code instructions would be required for each high level language instruction.

magnetic ink This is used when printing **characters** on forms which can be automatically read or sorted by machine as well as by people. The characters are distinctive in that they are made up of thick and thin lines.

For example, the numbers along the bottom of each bank cheque are printed in magnetic ink. On receipt of a completed cheque the bank staff

1 2 3 4 5
6 7 8 9 0

magnetic ink

type the amount onto the cheque itself in
magnetic ink and using a **magnetic ink character reader** linked to a computer all the necessary calculations and deductions are carried out
automatically.

magnetic memory Just as a bar of iron can be
magnetized with a north pole at one end and a
south at the other or the other way round so
other magnetic materials can be magnetized in
two ways. This is used to represent a 0 or a 1 and
is thus able to store **characters** in **binary
notation**. Magnetic **core store** consists of tiny
iron-type washers half a millimetre in diameter
wired in sets of 1024 (32×32) giving 1 K of
memory. Magnetic **tape** or card using several
tracks can hold over 1000 characters per inch
and transmit several inches worth to a computer
per second. Magnetic **disks** may be hard (rigid)

or floppy (flexible) and store characters on concentric tracks. Hard disks may be arranged in sets of say six, such a pack being removable from the **disk unit** or as a single disk in the case of a **Winchester disk drive**. Whereas floppy disks would hold hundreds of **kilobytes**, hard disks hold many megabytes (mega=million).

magnetic strip A small band of magnetic material across the back of a plastic card, shop tag or intercity rail ticket. **Data** can be magnetically encoded as a series of **binary digits**. Limited storage of approximately 64 **characters** means only main essential details can be encoded, for example, sorting codes and account numbers on bank cards, or product numbers on shop tags.

mail merge The selective merging of two **files** to produce a third. Within a **word processor** this may be used to personalize letters by merging names, addresses and other relevant **data** in turn from one file with a letter held as another file to produce a third which is printed.

main frame The **central processing unit** (CPU) of a large computer which has many **terminals**. Originally the words referred to the framework used to hold the CPU and **arithmetical logic unit** (ALU).

main store The **memory** of the computer that can be accessed immediately. **Core store** and **solid state** memory are used for the main store whilst magnetic **tape** and **disk** are used as **backing store**. Also called **immediate access store**.

maintenance contract Most computer manufacturers and computer repair companies offer service contracts on equipment. Such contracts may include preventive maintenance whereby the machine is serviced regularly in addition to guaranteed call-out times (i.e. the engineer will visit four times each year and within 24 hours of a fault being reported). Some maintenance contracts include labour charges but not the cost of replacement parts: a full service contract would include both.

mark sense cards Computer cards (which may be **punched cards**) divided into columns allow-

mark sense cards

ing spaces for marking with a pencil line (mark sense forms are also available). These marks can then be read electrically by a machine (mark sense reader) linked to a computer or **card punch**. This is similar to optical scanning where the marks are read by a light-sensor. Both methods are useful for collecting and analysing responses to multiple-choice type questions.

master file The file that holds the latest version and from which working files are copied for everyday use. It is always available should a working file copy go wrong though normally it is only used when it is being updated from the working file.

matrix printer See **dot matrix printer**.

media All materials used to hold **data**. Computing examples would include magnetic **disk**, **optical disc** and **continuous stationery**.

mega/megabyte Mega is the prefix which normally denotes a million, but which in computer terminology stands for two to the power 20, i.e. 1 048 576. So although a megabyte is actually 1 048 576 **bytes**, the term is increasingly being used to denote a million bytes.

memory A store for **data** or program instructions made up of the **main store** and its **backing store**. Sizes are measured in **bytes** and are given as so many K meaning kilobytes. For example, a 512 K RAM microcomputer.

memory mapping Items of **data** are often more easily accessed if they are stored in an **array**. However, the computer **memory** consists of **locations** one after the other, and data, though arranged in an array can be stored sequentially. The arranging or mapping of arrays in this way (in a 'known' part of the memory) takes less space than arrays created in a **high level language**. Memory mapping is also useful for sending data to peripherals, in particular to a **visual display unit** (VDU). Here data is made to appear on a **peripheral** device simply by putting it in a certain part of the **immediate access** memory.

memory switching system As its name implies this **communications** system uses a computer to accept messages from its **terminals**, stores them if necessary and then transmits them to other terminals as indicated by the message.

menu A screen list that is presented to the user with the alternatives labelled, for example A, B, C, D. The user can select by pressing one key.

merge The bringing together of two or more **files** to make one; it can be **software**-controlled where the merging is selective as in **mail merge**.

menu   A typical menu on a VDU.

microcomputer   A computer which uses a **microprocessor chip** such as the Motorola 6502, the Zilog Z80A or the Intel 80286 for its central processor.

microelectronics   That section of electronics which uses extremely small electronic parts. **Integrated circuits** are one example where cost, size, weight and power consumption have been reduced considerably, coupled with an increase in reliability.

microfiche   A photographic-like slide (or film in the case of 'microfilm') which is viewed using a special type of high magnification projector. Pages of print, diagrams and graphs are considerably reduced in size and stored in this way. A 6×4 inch microfiche could hold up to 250 pages whereas a continuous roll of microfilm might hold 2000 pages. Computer **output** can be directly put onto microfiche or microfilm using either a **cathode ray tube** (CRT) picture which is reduced in size or a special laser **printer**. In addition to the size there is a considerable weight reduction compared with printed paper output. With special machines a computer can select and read pages from microfilm.

microfloppy   At present the most popular form of magnetic **disk** for **microcomputers**. It consists of a 3.5 inch disk inside a hardened plastic case with a sliding cover which reveals the region accessed by the read/write heads of the microcomputer. It spins at around 300 revs per minute.

Data is recorded along concentric circle **tracks** divided into **sectors** and there are approximately 135 tracks per side. As the disk is rigid, data and tracks can be tightly packed together and the read/write heads can be very close to the surface. Consequently, microfloppies can have up to 1.4 **megabytes** capacity, far more than other floppies.

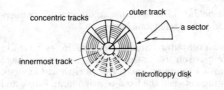

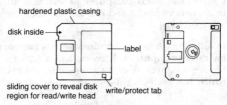

microfloppy A typical 3.5 inch disk

microprocessor A special LSI **chip** that is used as the **central processing unit** of a computer. It is able to receive and store **data**, perform arithmetical and logic operations according to its stored **program** and give out the results. In addition to **microcomputers** their use is so wide that it is difficult to suggest an area in which they will not be used. Applications today include cookers and washing machines, cars and aircraft, machine tool control and remote monitoring of oil fields, video machines, bank cash dispensers and public telephone boxes.

minicomputer Small-sized machines that, in comparison to **main frame** computers, have limited **memory** and a few **peripheral** devices. Being between the fixed-position main frame and the portable **microcomputer** its size is similar to a small wardrobe and is generally used to do one specific job.

minifloppy A form of **random access memory** for **microcomputers**. It consists of a 5.25 inch flexible magnetic **disk** inside a cardboard cover which has sections cut-away for the disk drive

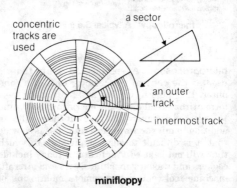

concentric
tracks are
used

a sector

an outer
track

innermost track

minifloppy

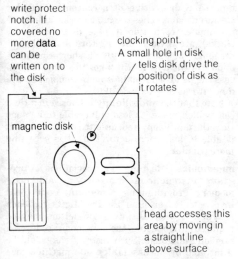

write protect notch. If covered no more **data** can be written on to the disk

clocking point. A small hole in disk tells disk drive the position of disk as it rotates

magnetic disk

head accesses this area by moving in a straight line above surface

minifloppy A disk in its cardboard holder.

unit (**disk unit**) and the read/write head to access the disk.

When spinning at around 300 revs per minute the disk is rigid and the head moves in a straight line between the centre and the edge. Just as a cassette **tape** recorder uses parallel tracks on a tape so a disk drive uses concentric circular tracks on a disk. These circular tracks, around 40 in number each side (double density has 80 tracks), are divided into **sectors** and although the length of track in a sector is shorter near the middle of the disk it still takes the same time to pass the head. Thus data is more compact on the inner tracks of a disk.

Note that the **microfloppy** is housed in a rigid case which makes it less vulnerable to damage than the minifloppy and, despite being smaller, it is able to hold more data. Thus it is becoming more popular.

mnemonics   Meaningful abbreviations for **program instructions** designed to aid one's memory. Programming in **machine code** could involve eight or nine **binary digits** for each instruction whereas only a few letters may be required when using the mnemonic code of a symbolic language. Such instructions would be translated by an **assembler** into machine code (one program instruction becoming one machine code instruction) so that it can be understood and run by the computer.

For example,

> CLA meaning CLear **Accumulator**
> DIV   meaning DIVide

though in this case the **programmer** would also have to specify what it was that had to be divided (the **operand**); this too could be a letter instead of an **address** number.

mode The way in which the particular piece of equipment has been set up. It may refer to the resolution of the graphics on the **screen**, or the type of output that is being provided. For example, 'graphics mode', 'serial mode'.

modelling The manipulation and investigation of a computer model of a real or imaginary situation. This allows the user to try out various alternatives ('what if') within the safety of a computer system.

modem A device which enables **data** to be sent long distances over the telephone lines. The 0s and 1s representing the data are used to affect the wave form that travels along the wire, thus it carries the coding. This is called **modulation** and the word modem is an **acronym** for the two words **MO**dulator/**DEM**odulator.

For example, two computers each connected via a modem (British Telecom approved) to the telephone line are able to transfer programs and data at high speed (of the order of several thousand **baud**). An alternative method would be to use an acoustic coupler which uses an ordinary telephone.

modulation The technique of using **data** signals to modify a transmitted wave so that the wave carries the data signals. There are three ways in which a wave can be affected: by changing its amplitude (size), or its frequency or its phase. By varying one of these using a **modem** a data **signal** can be superimposed on a carrier wave.

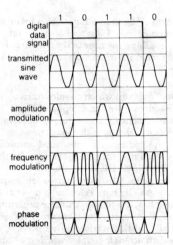

modulation Types of modulation.

module A part of a **program** or **applications package** that is complete in itself though may call upon **data** from other modules. In producing a complete program, several modules are joined together.

modulus A constant value used to divide other numbers to ascertain the remainder.

For example,

11 divided by mod 7 = remainder 4.

Moduli are used in **check digit** operations.

monitor 1. Most **microcomputers** can display their **output** on a television set, the **signal** being accepted via the aerial socket. For better definition, particularly with graphics, a monitor is required which accepts a **video** signal. This signal has a lower frequency though can be either black and white or colour. In addition there are R.G.B. monitors which accept separate signals for the three colours, red, green and blue, which make up the picture on a colour **screen**.
2. Any device or a part of the operating system that examines what is happening in a computer system and takes action if something is wrong.

monochrome Using only one colour, usually white on a black screen though green and sometimes orange are also used. **Inverse video** uses the reverse: black on a coloured screen.

most significant character The **character** on the extreme left of a set of characters.

mother board Some **microcomputers** consist of more than one **printed circuit board**. There may be a board to control access to the **disk drives**; one to provide **high resolution graphics**; one for colour; one to support the input/**output** user **ports**, and so on. The board that holds and supports all the other boards is known as the mother board. Sometimes this also holds the **microprocessor** and thus controls access to the other boards. However there are computers with only one board (single-board computers) and computers contained on a single **chip** (microcontroller).

mouse A desktop device which has a ball underneath. When moved about, it relays speed and direction and so guides a pointer across the

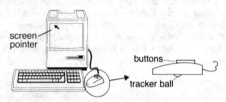

screen
pointer

buttons

tracker ball

mouse The mouse is connected by a cable to its PC.

screen. It reduces the need for **keyboard** instructions as the pointer can be directed to an **icon** (a pictorial symbol) and functions can be selected by using the buttons on its top. The mouse is part of the **WIMP environment** and is also extensively used in Computer Aided Design (CAD), word processing and graphics programs.

MS-DOS A popular disk-operating system (DOS) produced by the Microsoft Corporation.

multi-access processing system Also called multi-user or **time-sharing** system, this consists of a central computer with a specialized **operating system**. Many users on **dumb terminals** can be linked to the central computer which polls (checks) each incoming line in turn. If a terminal

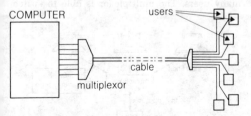

multi-access processing system The cable links terminals to the computer.

wants access to the CPU, **data** is transmitted from the **multiplexor** or attached **backing store**, down a fast input link to the CPU. The data is processed very quickly and returned. This is called roll in—roll out. Because of the speed with which each terminal line is polled and processed (**response time** is normally within five seconds), terminal users often think they have sole use of the computer.

Multi-access processing systems are used for single applications (often over large geographical areas) requiring central processing, for example: holiday/airline booking; the police national computer; the Inland Revenue tax system; and ATMs (automated teller machines or cash cards).

multiplexor A device which controls the transmission of **data** between a computer and its many users. The multiplexor is able to switch

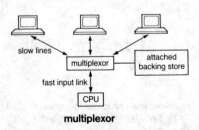

slow lines

multiplexor

attached backing store

fast input link

CPU

multiplexor

very quickly so that data along a single wire can be routed from or to many different wires each one behaving as if it had continuous contact. Often multiplexors are used in pairs some distance apart, each having many connections though only one path exists between them. This might be of wire, glass fibre or microwaves.

multi-task processing A specialized **operating system** which allows several **programs** to be held in the computer's **memory** at the same time. The operating system works out a processing priority so that **peripherals** such as **printers** are kept busy while the CPU can do any processing/calculations required. It gives the appearance of doing all its jobs together, but in fact little bits of each job are being done one at a time.

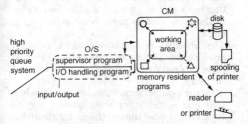

multi-task processing

The big advantage of **multi-task**ing is that all equipment, especially expensive peripherals, is kept busy most of the time, thus giving value for money. Additionally, printer 'spooling' gives the CPU more freedom to get on with processing other **data**. New types of multi-tasking **software** are now available, combining a specialized **operating system** with applications programs, for example Microsoft Windows, a **WIMP** set of programs.

multi-user system See **multi-access processing system**.

multivibrator A basic electronic circuit that can be built using two **transistors** and a few components. There are three types:
(a) The **astable** multivibrator which continuously switches from one of its two states to the other and is used in computers as a clock.
(b) The **bistable** multivibrator which rests in one or other of its two states and is used to store a **binary digit**. Sometimes known as a **flip-flop**.
(c) The monostable multivibrator which when switched to the other state always reverts back after a fixed time to the first state and is used for fixed timing or as a delay circuit.

musical instrument digital interface (MIDI)
This circuit provides a **digital output** and
accepts a digital input. Now found in all syn-
thesizers and electronic musical instruments and
having its own **programming language** that
enables up to 16 instruments to be 'chained' and
operated in any combination under the control of
a **microprocessor**.

N

NAND gate A logic gate, the same as **NOT
AND** (Not AND) whose **truth table** with two
inputs would be

Input		Output
0	0	1
0	1	1
1	0	1
1	1	0

NAND gate

It is worth noting that by joining the two inputs together on a NAND gate it becomes a **NOT** gate or an inverter:

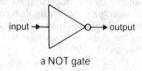

a NOT gate

Input	Output
0	1
1	0

nanosecond   One billionth (a thousand-millionth) of a second.

network   Networks allow **data** (which may be computer **programs**) to be sent over long distances between a set of computers. In a true network system each user is able to access all the facilities available on the system, the advantage being that they can all share the same **printer** and **backing store**.

neural network   A modern computer technology which is designed to resemble the nervous system of the brain. Just as the neuron cells conduct messages to and from the brain and learn by experience so the web-like structure of a neural network needs no programming and is suitable for computing tasks where logical rules are difficult to find (e.g. recognizing handwritten **characters**). Its strength lies in the number of interconnections rather than the processor speed.

noise This is often the cause of errors in **data** that have been transmitted via a telephone wire. Random changes in voltage, frequency or phase can cause a change in the **signal** being transmitted and this results in the wrong **code** arriving at the receiving end. This problem is greatly overcome by using **digital** signals for transmission.

non-equivalence gate (NEQ) A **logic gate** which operates with **binary digits** and is also known as the **exclusive-OR gate**. Its output is of logic value 0 only when all its inputs are the same. (Note that with an inclusive-OR gate the output is of logic value 1 when any of its inputs has a logic value 1.)

For example, with a two-input NEQ or X-OR gate the following **truth table** applies:

Input		Output
0	0	0
0	1	1
1	0	1
1	1	0

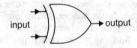

NEQ or X-OR gate

This gate could be used to find whether or not two binary digits are the same: it could also be used to sum two binary digits but it does not give the carry digit (i.e. when adding 1+1 in binary notation we get 10 where the 1 is the carry digit and the 0 is the sum).

NOR gate A **logic gate**, the same as **NOT OR** (Not OR) which operates with **binary digits**. Its **output** is of logic value 1 only when all its inputs have a logic value 0; otherwise it is 0.

For example, with a two-input NOR gate the following **truth table** applies:

Input		Output
0	0	1
0	1	0
1	0	0
1	1	0

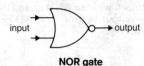

NOR gate

normalize When working with **floating point arithmetic** it is necessary to adjust each number so that it has the required number of **digits** after the point. The number is then said to be normalized.

NOT gate A **logic gate** sometimes known as an 'inverter'. The output is always the opposite of the input:

Input	Output
0	1
1	0

input → ▷o → output

NOT gate

When combined with an **AND** or an **OR gate** it inverts the output to give a **NAND** or a **NOR gate** respectively.

null string A **character** string that has nothing in it (e.g. "") not even a space. Used by **programmers**, for example, to denote the end of a **program run**. In **BASIC**, where the $ sign is used to indicate a string variable, a section of program (much simplified) might appear as:

```
1000 INPUT 'Please enter your name or press ENTER to finish', NAME$
1010 IF NAME$≠ "" THEN 2010
1020 PRINT 'Goodbye'
1030 END
```

where "" has nothing between the quotation marks.

numeric Referring to numbers. In **denary notation** this would mean the digits 0 to 9. A numeric **keyboard** would have 10 keys, one for each number.

numeric keypad A set of keys arranged in a block which are used for numeric input, though they may also have arithmetical functions.

numeric keypad

O

object code A **machine code** which the computer understands and which contains **data** as well as **instructions**. It is a binary version of a **high level language source program** and produced by a **compiler**, with or without an **assembler**.

octal notation In this system one counts in 'eights' instead of 'tens' using the digits 0 to 7. Whereas the three positions in denary represent hundreds, tens and units, in octal they represent 64s, 8s and 1s.

For example,

$$764 \text{ in octal} = (7 \times 64) + (6 \times 8) + (4 \times 1)$$
$$= 448 + 48 + 4$$
$$= 500 \text{ in denary}$$

To change from octal to binary notation each digit is converted in turn. 7 is 111, 6 is 110 and 4 is 100. So

$$764 \text{ in octal} = 111110100 \text{ in binary}$$
(Check $256 + 128 + 64 + 32 + 16 + 0 + 4 + 0 + 0 = 500$)

on/off line   Whether or not a **terminal** user is connected to the computer. Often terminals off line are used for **data** preparation though if they have their own processor they can operate as an independent computer.

open document architecture (ODA)   A set of standards aimed at facilitating mail and document connectivity between systems which support **text** and graphics.

open systems interconnect (OSI)   An ISO standard for **networks**. It has seven layers, each one responsible for a specific **communications** operation or hardware specification.

operand   The second part of a **machine code** instruction. In the first part the **programmer** puts an **operation code** that controls the process to be done (this might be to print, or to **load** the

accumulator). The operand controls which **memory locations** are used and, for example, to which port or device the data is to be sent. A machine code instruction using a 24-**bit word** might be arranged in 8 and 16 bits.

★★★★★★★★	★★★★★★★★★★★★★★★★
OPERATOR	OPERAND
8 bits	16 bits
255 processes	65 536 different addresses

operand   Operator and operand.

operating system The **program** which supervises and controls an entire computer system including all of its **peripherals**. It provides the link between the **hardware** and the **applications package** being **run**. All commonly used facilities are incorporated, including the saving and loading of **data** and programs, **disk unit** control, **memory** management and allocation, and the displaying of messages when necessary. **Security** features such as **passwords** and/or restricted access may be included, and large computer installations often have specialized operating systems which make the best use of the expensive equipment provided. A **job control language** consisting of commands and **instructions** allows the user to communicate with these operating programs. Popular operating systems include **MS-DOS**, **UNIX** and OS/2.

operation code The part of a **machine code** instruction which says what has to be done has, itself, to be coded. The code used is called the operation code and although it is in **numeric** form it would mean such things as 'print', 'add' and 'subtract'.

For example, the operation code for 'print' might be 13 and so to print the contents of **location** 17 a **programmer** might code

     1 3 0 0 1 7   or   13 17

However, in binary notation this would be

    00001101   0000000000010001

optical character reader (OCR) A device which is able to recognize normal **characters** like A, B, 6, ? and provide the corresponding input to a computer. At the present time such a

OCR Typical OCR characters.

machine would have difficulty in reading hand-writing though certain types of print are easily read.

optical disc These discs hold **data** digitally and are used to store computer data (also available as a good quality television sound and picture playback system, like a video tape). New **programs** and data are 'burnt' onto the disc surface as dips by a strong laser. It is read by detecting the changes in the reflected beam of a weaker laser which passes over the surface as the disc revolves. At present it is difficult to erase the contents and return to a perfectly smooth disc surface. The WORM (Write Once Read Many Times) technique overcomes this by writing new or revised data onto unused parts of the disc, thus giving the appearance of resaving programs or data. Since 12-inch discs have a 2 **gigabyte** capa-

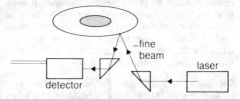

optical disc The detector reads the changes in the reflected laser beam.

city, it can be a long time before a disc is used up and a new one required. Currently 14-inch, 12-inch and 5.25-inch discs are available.

optical mark reader A means of detecting the presence or absence of a pencil mark in certain places on sheets of paper or computer cards. It is sometimes guided as to the positions to be read by clock marks (thick black lines) printed down one edge. Examinations Boards often use an optical mark reader to record candidates' answers to multiple-choice type questions.

Oracle The name of UK Independent Television's teletext service which transmits **data** along with the normal television programme transmissions. Each page is transmitted in turn in a never ending sequence as a form of 'dots' tucked away out of sight at the top of the television screen. With a **teletext** decoder this data can be made to fill the screen (or be superimposed over the picture) one page at a time. Oracle, in addition to providing sub-titles to some programmes, includes advertising pages and provides local information by transmitting a selection of different pages in different regions.

OR gate A **logic gate** which operates with **binary digits**. Its **output** is of logic value 1 when any of its inputs have logic value 1. With a two-input OR gate this **truth table** applies:

Input		Output
0	0	0
0	1	1
1	0	1
1	1	1

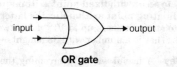

OR gate

This is the **inclusive-OR gate** as opposed to the **exclusive-OR** or **non-equivalence gate** which gives 0 if 'all' the inputs have logic value 1.

original equipment manufacturer (oem) One who makes and sells a piece of equipment which may include products of other manufacturers. Thus these others would point out that their products were suitable for use by an oem.

For example, the oem of a certain type of **printer** might use a print-head mechanism or an **integrated circuit** from another supplier.

output The available results of the computer's work: sheets and sheets of paper onto which the results have been printed or a picture on a television or **monitor screen**. Other examples of an output device include a graph plotter, **card punch** and **paper tape** punch and **microfiche**.

overflow A numerical answer which is too big for the computer to store in the space allowed. Generally a computer signals the problem to the user when this happens. Overflow is much more likely to occur with **fixed point arithmetic** than with **floating point arithmetic**, the latter being able to store numbers up to 10^{38} using two 8-bit words. That is a number with 38 noughts.

overlay A useful way of overcoming the problem of not having enough **main store** in a computer. The **program**, which is too long, is loaded and run in sections, more of the program being called into **memory** as and when required. Each new section overlays and rubs out a previous section.

overwrite 1. To replace **data** held in **memory** with new data.
2. An optional facility of **word processors** where typing new **characters** replaces existing characters.

P

Packet Switch Stream British Telecom's service which allows access via the telephone to various on-line services. Each service has its own exclusive network user address (NUA) and users must have their own network user identity (NUI). Some services (e.g. CAMPUS 2000) provide users with a common NUI within the subscription costs.

packing density A measure of the amount of **data** that can be held by a **backing store** usually stated as so many **bytes** or so many **bits** per unit length, **track** or **disk sector**. For example, 800 bits per inch for half-inch magnetic **tape**, or 500 bytes per sector.

page 1. A full **screen** of **data** as displayed by a **monitor**, though sometimes, as with **Prestel**, each full screen is called a **frame** and a page consists of several frames.
2. To switch between blocks of computer **memory**; *radiopaging* is a telecom service.

pagination Inserting page-breaks within a document. Within a **word processor** it can be done automatically or under the control of the user. When shown on the **screen**, page-breaks that split sentences or put the last line of a paragraph at the top of the next **page**, can be adjusted.

paper tape Computer paper **tape** is usually 2.5 centimetres wide and comes in rolls 250 metres long. It is punched, one **character** at a time, with a row of holes: four rows per centimetre length. Each row has the same number of possible holes which can be 5, 6, 7 or 8. Eight-track tape is divided 5 to 3 by the **sprocket holes** which are punched at the same time and are used to guide the tape through the reader. Being off-centre the tape cannot be fed in upside down.

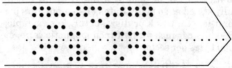

RETUPMOC SNILLOC

paper tape Examples of punched characters and spaces .

This type of coding can be read at 1500 characters per second by a paper tape reader.

parallel interface The circuit that provides a popular socket for connecting external devices to a **microcomputer**, for both output and input of **data**.

For example, an **8-bit** computer might have a parallel socket with eight wires or paths along which eight bits of data can be sent all at once. It might also have another eight wires for input.

parallel processing Conventional computers process **data** and **instructions** sequentially; they are brought in from central **memory** to the CPU, processed and then carried out. With parallel processing, **microprocessors** are wired in parallel, so processing takes place in many centres simultaneously. It is thought that this is how the human brain can do so many ordinary yet complex tasks. A cube of microprocessors together can deliver 40–50 mips (million instructions per second). This is supercomputer performance housed in a **microcomputer**. Applications requiring such power include weather forecasting and gigantic number crunching operations. At present, the leading parallel processor is the INMOS Transputer.

parallel transmission This requires at least as many wires or paths as there are **bits** to be transmitted at the same time, and this is what happens within and between the **integrated circuits** in a computer. With eight-bit **words** all the eight bits of each word would be transferred in parallel along eight paths simultaneously.

For example, imagine six rows of soldiers, with each row having eight men. To move this block forward each row could move in turn, eight men moving 'parallel' to one another.

```
........              first row/8 bits
↑
  ↑
........              second row/8 bits
........              third row
........              and
........                        so
........                          on
```

Alternatively, the man at the left of the first row could lead and his row could follow immediately behind him, with the second row doing likewise and so on, in line or 'serially'. This is the method used where all the bits need to go along one line, such as a telephone link or similar. Conversion from parallel to serial is handled by a **serial interface**.

```
    ↑ .
      .
      .
      .
  ↑ ...←
  ........              first row/8 bits
  ........              second row/8 bits
  ........              third row and so on
```

Both systems would use **parity bit** checks and **handshake** when outputting to other equipment.

parameter A value which has a particular meaning. Often in the course of carrying out a **program** (or a procedure) the computer does different tasks depending on the value of something or on the particular key that was last pressed.

parity bit An extra **bit** included with a set of **binary digits** as a check to see that all the binary digits are transferred correctly. Its value is 0 or 1 depending on the values of the other digits. If the number of 1s, including the parity bit, is even then the word has even parity: if the number of 1s is odd then it has odd parity.

PASCAL 1. **Pascal, Blaise** (1623–1662). A French mathematician who in 1642 designed and built a toothed gear-wheel machine that could do both addition and subtraction. This was the first mechanical **calculator**.
2. A **high level** programming **language** developed in the early 1970s as a teaching language. Today it is used for general purpose programming.

password A group of **characters** required to be given correctly when demanded by a computer before it will allow access by the user.

patch   A small program alteration written to overcome a minor error or unforseen circumstance and added to the main program.

peripheral   Any device that is connected to, and controlled by, a computer but external to the **Central Processing Unit** (CPU).

For example, **card reader**, **disk drive**, **bar code** reader, **joy stick** and games paddle.

personal computer   An alternative name for a **microcomputer**. The initials, PC, are generally taken to indicate an IBM personal computer or one that is **compatible**.

phone-back   See **security**.

photolithography   See **thin film memories**.

pitch   The number of **characters** per inch. In terms of printing this might be, for example, 10, 12, or 15.

pixel   These are the tiny areas (dots) that make up a computer graphics picture. The smaller each pixel, the greater their number and thus the higher the resolution of the picture (more detail can be seen). However, the variation in resolution and the number of colours depend on the **bits** per pixel. Thus **high resolution graphics** is accompanied by a reduction in the number of shades available.

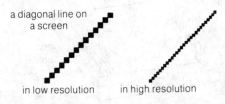

a diagonal line on a screen

in low resolution

in high resolution

pixel The smaller each pixel the higher the resolution.

For example, on a **monitor screen** 1280 by 960 pixels may allow only two colours (B & W), 1280 by 480 pixels might allow four colours, and 640 by 480 some 16 colours, whereas 320 by 480 pixels could allow as many as 256 colours.

platen As on a typewriter, the part of the printer against which the paper is pressed when printing takes place.

plotter An instrument for drawing lines on paper, often used to draw the two dimensional graphic **output** from a computer. On some instruments the pen is able to move in two directions; on others the pen moves in one direction and the paper is moved at right angles. Another method is to have the paper fixed to a cylinder

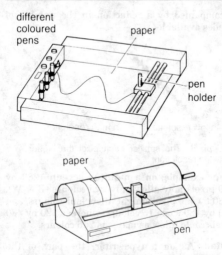

different
coloured
pens

paper

pen
holder

paper

pen

plotter Some plotters allow the paper holder to move back and forth in one direction and the pen to move at right angles (top); a *drum* plotter has the paper fixed to a rotating drum (bottom).

which revolves back and forwards while the pen moves sideways. Movement is generally done by stepping motors. Colour is achieved by using several (say four) different coloured pens, the carrier which moves selecting the right pen at the right time.

X-Y type. Here the values of X and Y positions are fed by the computer to the plotter as coordinates which are plotted by the pens.

Incremental type. As opposed to an X-Y plotter which requires X and Y values, this unit plots or draws according to **data** supplied by the computer, which moves it from its current position. Each plot is therefore relative to the previous one and not to a fixed origin.

point of sale (POS) The place in a shop or wholesale suppliers where the goods change hands. When you pay at the till the item becomes yours and any record, such as a stock control figure, needs to be changed at this point. A point-of-sale terminal may have its own **backing store** (e.g. magnetic cassette tape) or may be directly connected to a computer. See also **Electronic Funds Transfer at Point of Sale.**

polling Checking the status of different **ports** or **circuits** in order, so that time is allocated to each one in turn (only one is actually connected at any one time). Generally the user is not aware of this because it happens several times a second and does not seem to interrupt the work.

For example, with several users (multi-access) or several **programs** running (multi-tasking), the **microprocessor** has to poll each one in turn and if necessary continue execution for a short time before moving on to the next.

port   The plug or socket on a computer where **peripherals** are connected. If a change in the form of **signal** is necessary then an **interface** will be incorporated. Taken from the similarity with a ship coming in to load or unload.

portability   The ability of **software** to **run** on different machines with little modification.

Prestel   The name of British Telecom's **view-data** service designed for the home market with use during the evenings and weekends when telephone lines are less busy. At present, it is mainly used by businesses, but education users can obtain access through CAMPUS 2000. Signals travel from one of the Prestel computers (all of which are linked) via telephone line to a Prestel decoder and screen. Nearly 200 000 different pages are available and these cover topics as wide apart as the selection of wines and British Rail train timetables. **Information** providers (IPs) buy pages to display their goods or information. Users have to pay both telephone line charge and computer time charge and sometimes a **page** charge which is collected by British Telecom for the Information Providers. Most pages have a zero charge and it is possible to access other private viewdata systems through

Prestel. Some pages consist of computer **software** and by connecting a **microcomputer** via a British Telecom approved **modem** one can access this **telesoftware** as well as other Prestel pages.

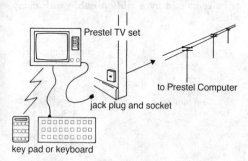

Prestel TV set

to Prestel Computer

jack plug and socket

key pad or keyboard

Prestel The user can communicate with Prestel via either a keypad or keyboard.

printed circuit board A thin board on which electronic components are fixed by solder. Sometimes the component wires are pushed through from one side and soldered on the other side which has the printed circuit, though often they are surface mounted. The printed circuit consists of metal strips which connect one component to another. Several such boards would be used in a **microcomputer**, one having the

microprocessor, another having sets of **memory chips** and others for **high resolution graphics** or controlling the **disk** drives. Such a set of boards might all plug into a **mother board** or be connected by a **ribbon cable** with many wires.

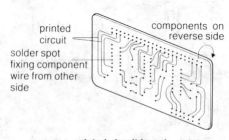

printed circuit

components on reverse side

solder spot fixing component wire from other side

printed circuit board

Note that many more intricate connections are possible with a printed circuit board than with a wired circuit. In fact double-sided printed circuit boards are also available.

printer This device or **peripheral** is used to obtain **hard copy** of the **output** from a computer. It can be either a mechanical (or impact) printer or a non-impact printer. Impact printers include: **dot matrix**, band, belt, thimble, or **daisywheel** machines. They are noisier and slower but have the advantage of being able to produce carbon copies while they print. Non-impact printers use thermal, **electrostatic**, **laser**, **ink-jet** or **magnetic ink** techniques. The most popular printers at the moment are the dot matrix. The relative speeds of some printers are:

daisywheel printer	50 cps
dot matrix printer	120 cps
ink jet printer	240 cps
line printer	1000 lpm
laser printer	10 ppm

(cps = characters per second, lpm = lines per minute and ppm = pages per minute)

printout The printed sheet(s) that the **printer** produces as a result of a computer **output**. This might be just one line of **characters** or several hundred pages of **text**.

program The set of **instructions** which the computer carries out. In whatever language the program is written the machine follows the instructions one at a time in order. There are five main steps in writing a program:

(a) Understanding and solving the problem;
(b) **Flow chart** or plan of the solution;
(c) Coding the program;
(d) Writing the documentation;
(e) Trials for testing.

With a **top-down** approach to **structured programming** the first three steps would be applied to sections at a time resulting in a set of programs each having a particular problem to solve.

programmable read only memory (PROM) This is similar to a ROM **chip** whose non-**volatile memory** is used to store a fixed **program**. Using a special hardware device it is possible to create one's own ROM using a PROM, but unlike an **EPROM** it cannot then be changed.

program maintenance The checking and changing necessary to keep a **program** in proper use.

For example, making changes due to the VAT rate being modified by the Government, adding a previously missed facility, speeding up a frequently used **routine**. It is important that program writers design their programs for easy maintenance.

programmed learning A planned learning sequence with alternative routes that allow self-study at one's own rate. At each **branch** the direction to the next piece of work can be based on the results or answers to the questions of the previous piece. Although never very widely used as much as a conventional paper-based scheme, computers have brought to the student the

prompt

seudo-random sequence of numbers When
ie computer is asked to generate a **random**
umber it does so by carrying out a set of
astructions. The numbers produced can be
ken as random but it is possible to repeat the
'ocess starting in the same way and to obtain
ie same set of random numbers. Only if one can
.volve some other changing factor, such as the
me' since switching on, can this be partly
ercome.

ablic domain software Free software or soft-
are available for a small fee.

ll-down menu A facility that is available as
list of options with some software packages.
ith a **mouse**, clicking on an **icon** at the top of
e **screen** and moving downwards results in the
·nu (of options) being 'pulled down'.

advantage of an interactive **medium** capab
storing the progress made and presenting
right piece of work at the right time.

With the advent of **compact discs** and op
discs providing moving pictures and
access to a large number of stillframes,
method of training and learning is becc
more popular.

programmer The person who writes the
puter **program**. More specifically the on
encodes the **algorithm**, which has been de
by the analyst, in a specific **program
language**.

programming language The language
allows the computer user to tell the co
what to do. There are many different lan
some of which are mentioned in this
Under the general heading of **high
languages** one might include A
FORTRAN, COBOL, BASIC and PA
Machine code or the manufacturer's
bler would be **low level languages**.

prompt A message which the computer
its operator. It may be a symbol (e.g.
sentence on a **screen** or a coloured ligh
keyboard (see overleaf).

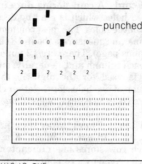

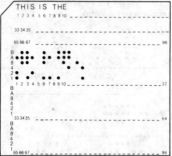

punched card The 80-column card which uses the 12-bit Hollerith code (top), and a 96-column card (bottom).

punched card A card storing **data** in the form of punched holes which is read by detecting the positions of the holes. The most common card has 80 columns and measures about 18 cm by 8 cm (see previous page). There are 12 punching positions in each column and, generally, one particular hole is used for the digits 0 to 9 and a combination of two holes for the other characters. A few card codes use three holes in one column.

punched tape **Paper tape** after it has been punched. As with each column on a **punched card**, each row stores one **character**. A paper tape punch driven by a computer can punch up to 100 characters per second.

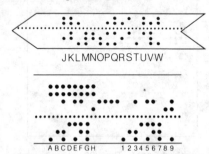

JKLMNOPQRSTUVW

ABCDEFGH   123456789

punched tape 5-track tape and 8-track tape.

Q

query language A language specifically designed to assist the user to interrogate a particular **database** and easily produce reports with **graphics** with a simple query.

queue A list or line of **data**, where new items are added at one end and the items are taken from the other. For example, a **printer** queue where users on a network send their work to the same printer, and each has to queue for its turn to be printed.

QWERTY The **keyboard** on a normal two-handed typewriter. The word comes from the first six keys on the second row of the keyboard:

It is interesting to note that the layout of the keys was designed not for speed as we might wish today, but for the opposite reason. Letters used often were positioned so as to allow time for the hammer to fall back to its place without being hit by the hammer of the next **character**.

R

random access memory (RAM) A set of storage **locations** any of which can be accessed directly without having to work through from the first one. Such memories can be both written to and read from and access times are about the same for all locations. We tend to think of **semiconductor** memories as being the equivalent RAM to **core store** though moving **magnetic memories** such as **disk** and drum are also RAM but have greater access times. Semiconductor RAM can be based on the junction transistor or the field effect transistor (TTL or CMOS). The first offers the faster access but the latter offers both dynamic RAM and static RAM; dynamic is the cheaper but requires extra logic circuits to check the contents regularly.

random numbers A set of numbers each one picked entirely by chance. This is not truly possible with most machines and we talk of a **pseudo-random sequence of numbers** being produced by a **microcomputer**.

range checks See **validation**.

raster scan The set of lines made by the electron beam of a **cathode ray tube** as it sweeps across the **screen**. Note that the beam scans the screen twice, each time covering every other line. The three international systems NTSC in USA, PAL in Britain and most of Europe and SECAM in France have a different number of lines scanned at different speeds.

read only memory (ROM) A **memory** that holds **data** or **instructions** permanently and cannot be altered by the computer or **programmer**. The actual content of a ROM is fixed at the time of its manufacture (PROM is fixed using a special device by the user; EPROM can be changed with difficulty by the user).

For example, a **semiconductor** ROM can be used to store **BASIC** in a **microcomputer** or to store the control **programs** in pocket **calculators** and other hand-held devices.

read/write memory This type of **memory** can be written into, as well as read, as opposed to read only memory (ROM). It might be **random access memory** (RAM) or a random access **disk file**, but **serial access memory**, such as **bubble memory** and magnetic **tape**, would also be included.

real time processing The use of a computer system to retrieve **data** and update the records at that time (in real time) feeding back results almost immediately and so changing the source of the data. This is unlike a **point-of-sale backing store** which may only be accessed by the computer once a day.

For example, an airline booking system is accessed by remote **terminals**. On receiving a booking the operator checks that it is available and if so updates the records and confirms the acceptance. From that time other users will find that booking is not available.

re-boot A term instructing the user to load the system again. Often used when the **program** has gone wrong or is in an endless **loop** from which it cannot leave. Also used as a way of changing the program stored in a **microcomputer**: re-boot and re-load.

record Each entry in a **database**. Each record consists of entries in a number of **fields** and a collection of records forms a **file**.

	AD. No.	FIRST NAME	SURNAME	DOB
Record 1→	6371	SUE	COLLINS	031064
	6592	DEBBIE	JANES	070666
	4217	PHILIP	JONES	270272
Record 4→	7631	MARK	BYRNE	100965
	8210	JANE	COLLIER	250660

record A database can have several sets of files.

red, green, blue (RGB) A **video signal** system which uses three separate signals, one for each of these three colours, to produce a higher definition coloured **screen** image than can be achieved with a single composite signal. **Pixels** are individually activated by one of a **monitor**'s three scans of the electronic beam to produce the correct colour dot in the desired position.

reduced instruction set computer (RISC) A computer with a **microprocessor** that has programmed in it only the most frequently-used instructions. It is reckoned that for most users 80% of their time is spent using only 20% of the microprocessor's instruction set. In the RISC the fundamental instructions are used as building blocks and combined to form more complex tasks. The aim is to obtain the maximum speed at which an instruction can be executed. RISCs have speeds of 3 mips (3 million instructions per second) and upwards. This contrasts with **Complex Instruction Set Computer** (CISC) microprocessors where complexities result in slowness of operation. RISC microprocessors can also **emulate** instruction sets of different computers. Existing **software** will run many times faster, and it is easy to **port** (transfer) **high level languages** like **Pascal** and C across many different computers.

refresh rate   The number of times per second that the **data** held in a dynamic RAM **chip** or on a **screen** display must receive a 'booster' signal to maintain its accuracy or visibility.

register   A special type of store **location** in a computer used for a specific purpose. Generally a register is the same size as the **word**-length of the computer.

For example, one register might be used as the **accumulator**; another as the **store address register**.

relative addressing   See **address**.

remote control At present such devices are used to operate television receivers, video recorders and some **Prestel** sets. Using a weak infra-red beam (like a light beam but one that is not detected by our eyes) these gadgets enable a person to operate the machine from various distances with a hand-held keypad. In a similar way one could operate a computer from the comfort of an arm-chair.

requirements report This follows the **feasibility study** in the development of a new **applications package** but precedes the design, implementation and review stages.

re-run To run the computer **program** again with the original **data** starting from the beginning.

reserved word Generally a word which has a specific meaning to the **compiler** or the operating system and thus must not be used by the **programmer** when programming in the **high level language**.

reset Sending a **signal** to the **microprocessor** which causes it to restart as if it had just been switched on, with all the **registers** being reset to zero. Some **microcomputers** have a **BREAK** key for this purpose, some a reset button, whilst others require the user to press three keys at the same time.

response time   The time taken for a computer to answer after the last key is pressed. This time seems very short in the case of a **micro-computer** but can vary greatly when accessing a main frame computer from a **terminal**. The time includes transmission, coding and decoding, in both directions and would depend on the number of other users. Short response times are particularly desirable for **multi-access processing** systems, two seconds maximum often being part of the specification.

ribbon cable   An electrical cable which consists of many separate wires held together in a flat flexible casing. It is used particularly when a large number of wires is required.

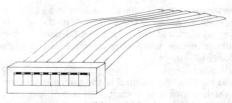

ribbon cable

right justification   1. The arranging of lines of

text so as to justify the right-hand edges and make them all in line.

2. Data stored in consecutive **locations** all of which have been filled from the right and may have a different number of spaces on the left.

right shift In this operation all the **characters** in a particular string are moved one place to the right. If a number is involved then this would have the effect of division.

For example, just as shifting a denary number one place to the right has the effect of dividing by 10 so a binary number is divided by two.

| in denary | 768.0 | becomes | 76.8 |
| in binary | 11010 (=26) | becomes | 1101 (=13) |

robotics Machine movement under the control of electronics or microelectronics which enables complicated and repetitive tasks to be carried out without further human involvement. It includes such devices as automatic welding machines and automatic warehouse cranes.

rogue value When **data**, such as a series of numbers, are being put into a computer an extra value is given at the end to show that there are no more numbers.

For example, when putting in a set of values which are the ages in years of a group of people, the value 999 might be used as the rogue value.

It must not be possible for the rogue value to
appear as one of the set.

rounding One way of reducing a number to a
certain number of **digits**. In **denary notation** if
the last digit removed from the right-hand side is
a 5 or above the last figure remaining is
increased by one.

For example, rounding the number 672.87 to
four figures would give 672.9; rounding to three
figures would give 673; to two figures would give
670. On the other hand **truncating** to four
figures would give 672.8.

routine A piece of **software** that does a specific
task though generally also part of a **program**.
However the word **subroutine** is often used to
describe a self-contained section of a program.

RS232, RS423 Code or name given to standard
interfaces for serial transmission of **data**. See
also **data communications**.

RUN A command to tell the computer to carry
out a **program**, though it can imply the loading,
the execution and the **output** of a whole package.
The 'run-time' is a measure of the time taken for
the whole program to be carried out.

S

scanner An input device that collects **data** by recording values of brightness for small areas (dots), as it moves across a surface. Used for digitizing ('reading') **text**, as well as pictures, into a computer.

scheduling The arranging of the order in which **programs** are to be **run**, which may be done by the computer itself.

For example, it may not be possible to run the first program in a **queue** if it requires more **memory** than is available at that time. Even programs that are running sometimes let others go ahead if a certain **peripheral**, say a **printer**, is not free when required.

schema An outline description or diagram of a **database** that can be accessed by the computer.

scratch pad memory An area of **memory** where the computer may hold results of calculations that it will need later, just as we might use a rough pad for working out, say, the cost of 24 pens at 17p each.

scratch pad memory

screen   The front of a television set, **visual display unit** (VDU) or **monitor** used for displaying computer text and graphics.

Screen copy is the output from a computer as seen on a screen;

Screen editor refers to the editing facilities offered to the user by a **terminal** screen;

Screen memory is the memory available to the computer or the user in the terminal itself.

scroll   The continuous movement of the display on the **screen** where generally as one line is added at the bottom all lines move up one and the line at the top disappears from view. Most **microcomputers** can be set to scroll either one page at a time (one screenful) or continuously. Horizontal scrolling is used with some **word processors**. Here, should the line length be greater than the screen width then on reaching the right-hand side of the screen the whole display moves to the left. Some **text editor** type **programs** only move the particular line to the left.

search To find particular items from a large set of **records**. The computer can do this very quickly; in a search, each item would be accessed and checked in turn by the **program** which would only select those required.

second generation computers These computers built between the mid 1950s and the mid 1960s used **transistors**. Thus they were smaller, more reliable and required less power than the **first generation computers** which used electronic valves.

second generation languages (2GL) These came about with the advent of **transistors** and are a step up from programming in **machine code**. 2GLs allow you to program using a function code (sometimes called a **mnemonic**, or memory aid) and a **location** showing where to find the **data**. Such languages became known as **assembly languages**. They depend on the type of CPU used, are tedious to program but are quickly converted and executed (**run**) by the assembler (translator). Examples are shown overleaf.

function code	location	
LDA	100	(load accumulator with contents of location 100)
ADD	101	(add contents of location 101)
STO	102	(store answer in location 102)

sector Part of a **disk** track. A magnetic disk or drum uses circular tracks for storing **data**. These tracks are **formatted** into sectors and the computer writes **data**, one sector track at a time, from its **memory**. Note that although the length of a track in a sector near the centre of a **minifloppy disk** is shorter it holds the same amount of data as those further out.

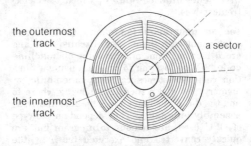

the outermost track

a sector

the innermost track

sector How a disk is divided into sectors.

security Measures to make something safe. In addition to the obvious physical security of computer systems, there is the problem of **data** security. This is threefold: data can be lost (e.g. during updating), wrongly modified (e.g. by an unauthorized user), and confidential data can be stolen (e.g. industrial espionage). The last two can usually be prevented by requiring passwords for access (more than one can be required each time) which are changed frequently, and also by *phone-back* where the remote computer has to return the telephone call before access can be made.

seed crystal A small single crystal which when held in its own supersaturated solution grows into a large crystal.

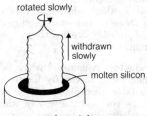

seed crystal

A small silicon seed crystal is rotated and

slowly withdrawn from molten **silicon** to give the cylindrical crystal from which silicon **wafers** are cut.

segment display A means of using **light-emitting diodes** and **liquid-crystal displays** to show the numbers 0 to 9. Generally the seven segments, a, b, c, d, e, f and g, lean slightly to the right.

segment display Note how segments combine to make the different numbers.

segmented program A computer **program** written in sections which are called up from **backing store** as and when required. One section would probably **overlay** the previous section in the main store.

semiconductor A material which is neither a good conductor of electricity like copper nor a good insulator like plastic. It is somewhere between the two and the way in which it conducts electricity can be changed by adding (called 'doping') a small amount of another substance (an impurity).

For example, **silicon** is a semiconductor; doping it with a small amount of arsenic provides extra negative electrons, giving what is known as n-type silicon; doping with phosphorous provides a lack of electrons giving p-type. Other semiconductors include germanium and the compound **gallium arsenide**.

sensor   An input device which measures values and provides **digital** readings for a computer system. It may record two states (e.g. light and dark), multistates (e.g. number of turns of a wheel) or **analogue** values (e.g. outside temperature).

serial access memory   This **read/write memory** is a set of **locations** which can only be accessed in sequence.

For example, to read a particular **record** stored on a magnetic **tape** it would be necessary to go through all the records in sequence until it is found. Another example is **bubble memory** though here **access times** would be shorter.

serial interface   The circuit that provides connection to a socket which transmits or receives each **bit** of **data** in order, one after the other.

shared files   Files held in the **memory** of one computer which can be read, used and altered by other computers to which it is linked either in a

network or by **telecommunications**.

The files are usually held in the **immediate access store** of a computer acting as a file server, or in **backing store** and can be called into main store when required.

shift register   The **location** in the computer which is used only for shifting **data** to the left or right. Note that a shift one place to the left of a denary number is like multiplying by 10, though the first digit of the number is lost if it filled the location completely.

For example, with a denary number:

> 0 4 7 2
> Shift left is like multiplying by 10:
> 4 7 2 0
> Shift right is like dividing by 10:
> 0 0 4 7

In **binary notation**:

> 0 1 1 0 (=6)
> Shift left is like multiplying by 2:
> 1 1 0 0 (=12)
> Shift right is like dividing by 2:
> 0 0 1 1 (=3)

signal   To convey **data** along a cable using electricity or through an electronic system. The change may be in the current flowing or the voltage used. In an **analogue** signal the change can have any value but with a **digital** signal there are only two values interpreted as 0 or 1.

For example, a common standard for serial transmission is RS232C where a 0 is less than −6 volts and a 1 is greater than +6 volts.

sign bit Usually the left-most **bit** in a **binary** number which indicates whether the number represented by the bits has a negative or positive value.

From this has evolved the *two's complement* method of representing numbers, which allows binary arithmetic to be performed in a manner suited to the electronic functioning of **digital computers**. Using this method, the left-most bit only (the *most significant bit*, or MSB, because it has the highest place value) has a negative value. If it is 'set' (i.e. 1) then because the rest of the bits together cannot add up to more than the MSB then the number represented will have a negative value. If it is not 'set' (i.e. 0) then the number represented will have a positive value.

For example, in eight-bit integer arithmetic:

```
Bit values are
 -128  +64  +32  +16  +8  +4  +2  +1
and
    0    1    0    0   0   0   0   1
is -0+64+1=+65

    1    0    1    1   1   1   1   1
is -128+63=-65
```

In **floating point arithmetic** a second eight-bit **word** for each number would give the position of the 'bicimal' point.

silicon A cheap and widely available **semiconductor** material that has replaced germanium in most electronic **solid state** devices. Although it is the second most abundant element (after oxygen) on the earth's surface it does not occur naturally. Sand and quartz are natural forms of silica (silicon dioxide) from which silicon is obtained.

silicon disk Also known as RAM disk, this is an extra RAM (**random access memory**) card which when inserted into the computer acts as a fast **disk** drive. A **utility program** is used to set up links to the CPU and modify the RAM area. Using a silicon disk can speed up, by five times or more, the loading, saving and operation of **application packages**. For some **software** a silicon disk is an essential requirement, particularly for those that use up memory very quickly.

Silicon Valley The region in California, USA where development of the **chip** took place and hence the manufacture of the first **microcomputers**.

simplex operation A mode of transmission that allows **data** to travel in only one direction.

A **terminal** that communicates with a computer via such a channel can either send or receive but not both. **Duplex operation** allows travel in both directions at the same time; half-duplex allows travel in both directions but not at the same time.

For example, simplex transmission could be from the **keyboard** of a terminal to its computer 'or' from the computer to the **visual display unit screen** of the terminal.

simulation   The representation of a situation by a computer system which allows the user's decisions and actions to cause the same effects and results as if being carried out for real. This assists training, particularly where mistakes in the real situation would be too costly or too dangerous. 'What if?' possibilities can thus be explored safely, quickly and cheaply.

For example, learning to fly a helicopter or operating a nucler power station, or forecasting probable profits and/or cash-flow in a commercial undertaking.

Sinclair, Clive   (1940–) British electronics engineer. He was the first to produce a widely available pocket calculator as well as a series of popular home computers.

small-scale integration (SSI)   See **large-scale integration**.

smartcard A plastic card, similar to a credit card, which has a **silicon chip** embedded in it, capable of storing, say, 64 **kilobytes** of **data** and **instructions**. The chip can store and communicate bank account details, credit/money transactions and personal information. A machine can be used to read and record data onto the chip via contact points. Any misuse of the card can be indicated and **stored**, resulting in card failure. The smartcard is used extensively in France and the USA for various purposes, and is expected to be in worldwide use in the 1990s. The smartcard contrasts with the **lasercard** which has a silver surface on which data is burnt as a series of dips.

soft-sectored The way in which the length of a **sector** is fixed on a **floppy disk**, the length being set by the **microcomputer** when the disk is **formatted**. **Soft-sectored** floppy disks have only a single hole near the centre hole of the disk whereas **hard-sectored** have a ring of say 6 or 12 (see diagram opposite).

softstrip A method of **data** storage where data is coded in **binary** as complex vertical black and white patterns on a strip of paper 24 centimetres long and 16 millimetres wide. Up to 5.5 **kilobytes** of data, in up to 10 **files**, can be held on a full length strip, and seven or eight strips

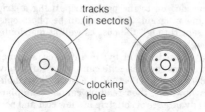

tracks
(in sectors)

clocking
hole

soft sectored   hard sectored

soft-sectored

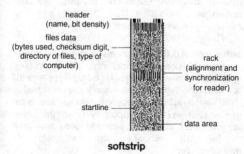

header
(name, bit density)

files data
(bytes used, checksum digit,
directory of files, type of
computer)

rack
(alignment and
synchronization
for reader)

startline

data area

softstrip

(approximately 40 kilobytes) can be printed on a
sheet of A4 paper.

Programs, **languages**, **text** and graphics can

be encoded on to the paper strip, using a strip-making program. Softstrips can be photocopied and sent through the post as well as distributed through magazines.

Data can be read by an infra-red **scanner**. This means that tea/coffee and other stains have no detrimental effect. If the strip is scribbled over, however, then reading cannot take place. The advantages of softstrip are low cost and portability, making it a good way of distributing data using a minimum amount of ordinary paper. It is at present being used for computer magazine (**public domain**) **software**, mailing lists and **database** distribution. Data distributed by this method is becoming known as stripware.

software   All the **programs** that can be run on a particular computer, including the **operating system**, the **assemblers**, the **compilers** and all the packages (specific programs for specific tasks) that are available. Software houses are companies that write and supply software packages for computer systems; thus one does not have to buy all software from the computer manufacturer.

solid state device   An electronic device that is made of solid material and has no moving parts. For example, transistors, **chips**, **core store**.

sort The arranging of items of **data** (e.g. a **file** of names or types of product) into a predetermined order. This might be alphabetical or numerical such as house number or date order. Sorting may be carried out on the whole file (thus every entry is then stored in sequence) or only on those items selected for printing. A computer sorts by comparing the items of data, two at a time and exchanging their positions in memory if necessary. Different methods of sorting (e.g. **bubble sort**, shell sort) make the comparisons in different order and sometimes the sort is only carried out on part of the record. **Inverted files** are sorted on a particular part of each record and although the sorting (*file inversion*) is very time consuming, in use such files are quickly accessed.

sound synthesizer The special electronic circuits, sometimes inside and part of a **microcomputer**, that can produce sound and imitate various musical instruments. Prior to 1983 these were usually **analogue**, but now are mostly **digital** which enables them to be connected to, and controlled by, a **microprocessor**. Linking to other apparatus is possible using the **musical instrument digital interface** system.

source language The language in which the **programmer** writes his **program** (the *source program*) though it cannot be directly understood by a computer. Either the source program is converted to an object program (**machine code** which can be run directly by the computer) using a **compiler** or it is **run** one line at a time using an **interpreter**.

For example, **BASIC**, **COBOL**, **ALGOL** are all source languages.

speech recognition The interpretation by the computer of the spoken word. Already in use are machines that respond to words though the vocabulary is limited and the pronunciation must be clear. Development at present is limited by processor speeds and **memory** sizes.

speech synthesizer The generation of speech by **solid state** circuits, used in hand-held educational machines and toys where a limited vocabulary is required. At present there is a noticeable difference between machine and human speech but more variation in machine accent is becoming available.

spell checker A facility offered by most word processing packages whereby a document is checked for wrongly spelt **words**. It does not indicate where a word has been wrongly used nor where a spelling error results in another different but correctly-spelt word, and therefore must be used with caution.

spooled file An acronym of 'Simultaneous

Peripheral **Operation** On-Line', this is one way of overcoming the problem of slow **peripheral** devices holding up the execution of a **program**.

For example, files to be printed are sent to a **disk** (fast transfer) where they join a **queue** and take their turn to be sent to the **printer** (slow transfer). See also **multi-task processing**.

spreadsheet program A **screen**-based representation of a large sheet of paper divided into rows and columns, each intersection containing a cell. **Text** can be entered as headings or labels for rows, columns, or groups of cells. **Data** entered in any cell or group of cells can be operated on by

	A	B	C	D	E	F	G	H	I	J
1					UNIT	TOTAL	UNIT	TOTAL		
2	ITEM	PRICE	DISC	SALES	REV	REVENUE	COST	COST	PROFIT	PER CENT
3		£	%		£	£	£	£	£	%
4	Pens	1.50	40	745	.90	670.50	.33	245.85	424.65	63.33
5		1.55	40	667	.93	620.31	.34	226.78	393.53	63.44
6		1.60	40	531	.96	509.76	.35	185.85	323.91	63.54
7	Clip pencils	1.25	40	830	.75	622.50	.27	224.10	398.40	64.00
8		1.35	40	775	.81	627.75	.28	217.00	410.75	65.43
9		1.45	40	689	.87	599.43	.29	199.81	399.62	66.67
10	A4 paper	1.35	40	927	.81	750.87	.30	278.10	472.77	62.96
11		1.45	40	824	.87	716.88	.31	255.44	461.44	64.37
12		1.50	40	732	.90	658.80	.32	234.24	424.56	64.44
13	A3 paper	1.55	40	597	.93	555.21	.35	208.95	346.26	62.37
14		1.60	40	523	.96	502.08	.36	188.28	313.80	62.50
15		1.65	40	412	.99	407.88	.37	152.44	255.44	62.63
16	A5 paper	1.00	40	995	.60	597.00	.25	248.75	348.25	58.33
17		1.15	40	836	.69	576.84	.26	217.36	359.48	62.32
18		1.30	40	774	.78	603.72	.27	208.98	394.74	65.38

spreadsheet program A typical example of a spreadsheet on hard copy.

formulae placed in other cells. By devising your own formula rules, individual cells or labelled groups of cells can be chained together to produce results. A change in any cell automatically triggers a chain of revised calculations and new results in other cells. Because of the computer's manipulative ability, spreadsheets are useful for problem-solving strategies and modelling of real-life events. Sometimes called 'what if' situations, spreadsheets can show the effects of changing events, circumstances or costs to the final results.

sprite A recognizable shape that can be designed by the user and moved around the **screen**. In turn these can be enlarged or reduced and brought together on one screen in a **graphical display**.

sprocket holes A series of holes along punched paper tape and along the edges of **continuous stationery**. In both cases they are used to feed the item automatically through a device. See also **tractor feed**.

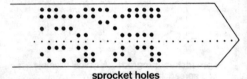

sprocket holes

stack 1. An area of **memory** used to hold temporary **data**. As each item is added the previous ones are all shifted down one place — thus they are thought of as being 'stacked' one above the other. New items are added at the end (top) and usually only the end one is removed at any time (i.e last in first out), although 'swopping' of the top two items can be performed.
2. Also used in the design of active learning packages where information is stacked, enabling the user to go deeper into the subject content if they so wish.

stationery Computer stationery is usually of the **continuous stationery** type which consists of fan-folded pages joined by perforations and having **sprocket holes** along the edges. These forms may be pre-printed with the name of the company or organization, leaving space on each page for the computer print. Sets of single sheets can be printed using single-sheet feeders.

stepping motor As opposed to an ordinary electric motor this turns a step at a time with, say, 96 steps for one revolution. The number of steps is fixed by the manufacturer and depends on both the number of sets of coils and the number of coils in each set. With four sets each having 12 coils, 48 positions are possible and 96 steps can be achieved by holding half-way between positions. It is moved from one position to another by activating different sets of coils in turn, using a sequence of numbers which can be provided by the digital **output** of a computer. This is an important method of producing precise movement under microprocessor control and is widely used in robotics.

stop bit Extra data included as part of the **handshake** to slow down transmission between computer and peripheral. It is used with serial rather than **parallel transmissions.**

store Anything that can retain **data** passed to it by the **central processing unit** of a computer. **Core store**, **memory chips**, **bubble memory**, magnetic **disk**, drum and tape are all types of store. The size of a store depends on the number of memory **locations**.

string A set of **characters** which may only be one character. Whereas numbers are stored in fixed length memories, the spaces being filled with zeros, characters are used in groups of various lengths. They are stored in a series of **memory locations** with the first location holding a number giving the length of the string (the number of characters). **BASIC** uses the dollar ($) symbol next to the **variable** to denote that it is a string.

For example, A$='HELLO' and this word might be stored in six locations, the first holding the number 5.

stripware Data stored or distributed on **softstrip**.

structured programming The art of writing **programs** that are logical and easy to follow. It involves the sectioning of the original problem into small program units each of which is self-contained and can be tested separately. The main program can then consist of a series of **instructions** each sending the computer to a particular unit or **subroutine** which it carries out and then returns. In addition instructions such as FOR ... NEXT, REPEAT ... UNTIL and DO ... WHILE ... allow easy structuring in program writing. With a **top down** approach the program is written in units in the same way as the problem was originally solved and it can be argued that **flowcharts** are not required with this method. However, the programming needs to be extremely well structured to work first time without them.

subroutine A section of a **program** written to carry out a specific task which the main program may use just once or several times during its run. The last instruction of a subroutine usually returns the computer to the one following the one from which it left the main program. Large computer systems have a set of subroutines on **disk** or tape which can be 'called' and used by the current program as and when required. A 'procedure' is a form of subroutine in that the **programmer** can use it once or several times during a program. The main difference is that it is 'called' by name and must be defined (written) outside the main body of the program. It can also have its own **variables**.

subscript 1. Characters (usually smaller) which are printed lower than the normal characters, e.g. the 2 in H_2O.
2. Subscript also refers to the second characters used to distinguish between similar variables (e.g. the numbers in A1, A2, A3).

superscript Characters (usually smaller) which are printed higher than the normal characters, e.g. the 2 in x^2.

synchronous mode The performance of a computer whereby the start of every operation is dependent on a pulse from its internal clock. Thus the completion of one task does not signal the start of the next as in **asynchronous mode** — the machine waits, albeit for a fraction of a second, for the next clock pulse.

syntax Rules to help understanding. Just as

the words we speak or write need to be in a certain grammatical order to be understood, so the **instructions** to a computer must obey certain rules. 'Syntax error' is stated by the machine when instruction errors have been made by the **programmer**.

For example, the instruction

10 INPUT A;B

in **BASIC** would give a syntax error because it should be

10 INPUT A,B

and the rules for writing **program** instructions have not been obeyed.

system The total of all the things that make up the working computer unit. It includes **hardware** (the computer itself plus all the **peripheral** units), **software** and the necessary **data** and operators.

system analysis The evaluation coupled if necessary with the design and installation of a computer system to solve a problem. Several stages are involved:
(a) Analysis of how the job is done at present.
(b) Deciding if a computer can be of use.
(c) Breaking down the problem into logical steps, designing a solution and specifying exactly what the computer must do.

(d) Installing the computer system and seeing that it works as required.

system flowcharts Charts used by systems analysts to understand, design and pinpoint the flow of work in a computer system. The flowchart can be used in planning and specifying particular **programs** that need developing. See also **flowcharts**.

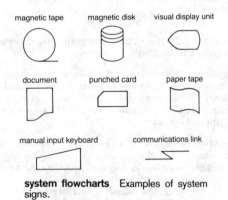

magnetic tape   magnetic disk   visual display unit

document   punched card   paper tape

manual input keyboard   communications link

system flowcharts   Examples of system signs.

System X British Telecom's digital telecommunications system. Speech from a telephone is table   199

converted into digital **data** (0s and 1s) and these digital **signals** are transmitted, as opposed to the continuously varying **analogue** signals as at present. Such signals can also be sent via **fibre optics** cables.

T

table The arrangement of **data** in rows and columns. In scientific work, it is a means of recording results from experiments in a way which allows different results to be related to one another.

Temperature/°C	Time/s
72	0
60	30
51	60
44	90
38	120
33	150

table This example shows temperature and time readings as a liquid cools.

Such results could be stored as an **array** in a computer **memory** as:

(72,0) (60,30) (51,60) (44,90) and so on

In addition items in such a table can be easily located by means of a **look-up table** which directs the computer without it having to search every item.

tape   A long strip of paper or magnetic coated plastic which is used to record **data**. Paper tape can use between five and eight holes to represent each character and half-inch magnetic tape similarly uses seven or nine channels across its width. (Audio cassette tape records **bits** serially one after the other.) One difference with magnetic tape is that data is usually stored in **blocks** and that in addition to checking the **parity bit** of each character the computer checks each block as it is read.

telecommunications   The sending of **data** from one place to another by radio waves or cables. Note the derivative of this word in the title 'British Telecom'.

teleprinter   Teleprinters and teletypewriters are devices similar to typewriters but with a limited **character** set. They were originally designed to send and receive code using **Telex** but are also used as computer terminals.

telesoftware Computer software transmitted from one computer to another by **telecommunications**. Telesoftware has been available on both the BBC's and IBA's **teletext** services and British Telecom's **Prestel** system, though radio transmissions have also been tried. Commercial and hobby *bulletin boards* also distribute software via the telephone and television services.

teletext An information service transmitted as part of the normal television signal. Each **page** is transmitted in turn in a never-ending

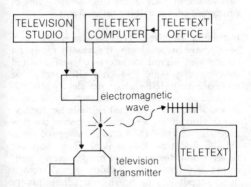

teletext The way in which the service reaches a user.

sequence as a form of 'dots' tucked away out of sight at the top of the television **screen**. If the receiving set is fitted with a teletext decoder these top four lines of the picture can be made to fill the whole screen. The user selects the page number and that page is decoded the next time it is transmitted. Information available varies from pages on news and sport to food prices and film reviews. In the United Kingdom the Independent Television Service's version of teletext is called **Oracle** and the BBC's is called **Ceefax**. Uses now include advertising, local information and various commercial information services, any of which may also distribute **telesoftware**.

television receiver The television set most people have in their home. It normally receives a transmitted **signal** via an aerial or cable and converts this radio frequency (RF) signal (or more precisely UHF signal) into picture plus colour and sound. Most **microcomputers** have a socket which gives a signal suitable for displaying the **output** on a television receiver but it is necessary to 'tune' the set to the required channel the first time this is done. Some sets are receiver/**monitor** and these have a second input socket which accepts a **video** signal from a microcomputer. This provides a better quality picture particularly when displaying detailed graphics. For the clearest quality colour picture the **red, green** and **blue** signals are sent separately and this requires an RGB computer output and an RGB monitor.

Telex   The service which allows users to communicate with each other using the telephone system and a **teleprinter**.

terminal   A device connected to a computer that allows input and **output** of **data**. A terminal may be just a **keyboard**, a teletypewriter (like a teleprinter) or a **visual display unit** (VDU) and is often remote from the computer.

For example, a magnetic stripe **card reader**, keyboard and display as in a bank cash dispenser or a **bar code** reader and cash till at a supermarket checkout. An intelligent terminal has its own processing power, a dumb terminal has not.

terminator   A false value, like a rogue value, attached to the end of a set of **data** and used to indicate to the computer that it is the last item. Similarly, terminators are used on **punched tape** to indicate the end of each record.

test data   Data run to try out a new program. Care must be taken to ensure that the test data covers all the possibilities, particularly where the user is given several choices and should include seemingly senseless entries that could be made inadvertently.

tetrabyte (Tbyte) The term for 1000 **gigabytes**, or 1024 **megabytes**, or a staggering 1 073 741 824 **bytes**.

text Letters, numbers and words as distinct from graphics and control codes.

thermal printer See **printer**.

thin film memories Integrated circuits (**chips**) made by depositing thin layers in patterns on top of one another. The chips on **silicon wafers** are built a layer at a time, the pattern of each layer being governed by a particular mask. The process by which ultra-violet light is used to define the pattern, and thus the circuit, is called *photolithography*. Today X-ray radiation and electron beams are used to define the pattern as with their smaller wavelengths more circuits and thus more memories are possible on the same size chip. See **X-ray lithography.**

third generation computers These were built using **integrated circuits**, the first in 1966. The second generation used **transistors** while the first generation used electronic valves.

third generation languages (3GL) Problem-solving languages, not dependent on the type of **Central Processing Unit** used, as were **second generation languages**. They came about with the introduction of **integrated circuits** and use commands/keywords which are near to English and have to be translated into **machine code** by either an **interpreter** or a **compiler**. These third generation languages (also known as **high level languages**) are good for general purpose programming, although some do specialize. They are widely used in education as well as for the development of code and they are portable across many computers.

Examples of 3GLs are:

        COBOL for business uses
        FORTRAN for scientific functions
        Pascal and C for structure and file handling
        Logo for list and database processing
        BASIC for general purposes

time sharing   When two or more users seem to be using the **computer** at the same time. In fact the computer is dealing with each in turn but to the individual user it seems that they have sole use. **Output** to a **printer** for one user though, could be printed at the same time as the computer does a calculation for another user. Only when the number of time-sharing users becomes large does the delay become noticeable. See also **multi-access processing system**.

top down   One method of programming whereby the **programmer** divides the problem into many small units each of which follows on from the one before. A computer **program** is then written for each of these units and tested separately. Only when it runs successfully is it added to the previous one. In this way the final program is built from the top downwards, and it is argued that no **flowchart** is required when using this method. However, **structured programming** is required for easy understanding.

touch screen   An input device that is able to record the position of a user's finger when touching the screen. It achieves this by either pressure on a resistive transparent material secured to the screen's surface, or by the interruption of vertical and horizontal light beams in front of the screen.

touch sensitive keys   Used for input, these keys have no moving parts. The pressure of the user's fingers or in some cases, just the electrical contact through the body to earth, is enough to make an input. Such **keyboards** have the advantage of being easily cleaned and can be liquid proof.

trace   A piece of **software** which follows each step of a **program** line by line. It enables the user to check and locate errors in programs by printing out each **location** as it carries out that instruction.

trace table The paper record provided by a trace **program** which is run at the same time as the user's program. Errors in the user's program can then be traced by studying this print-out, and put right before the program is released.

track The channel or line along which **data** is recorded on a storage device.

For example, the row of holes on **paper tape** or the magnetic line parallel to the edge on magnetic tape or **disk**.

tractor feed The method of moving paper through a **printer** (see overleaf). The advantage over **friction feed** is that when using pre-printed continuous stationery the lining-up of the paper and print is far more accurate.

Most small printers offer friction feed (the paper is held by the roller like a typewriter) but a tractor feed can be an optional extra.

transaction file This contains **data** which is used to update the **master file** and holds everything that has been changed since the last update. Often, such data is recorded in a transaction file as it is received in no particular order and transferred by **tape** or **disk** at a later time.

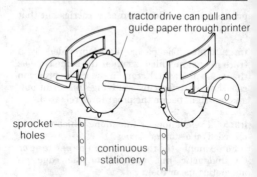

tractor drive can pull and
guide paper through printer

sprocket
holes

continuous
stationery

tractor feed The paper is held by the
sprocket holes along the two edges.

transducer Any device that converts energy
from an electrical form or to an electrical form.

For example, a loudspeaker is a transducer in
that it converts electrical energy into sound
energy that we can hear. Other examples include
a light sensitive pen in a bar code reader, an
electric motor, or an electrical thermometer.

transistor A semiconductor device. Invented in
1948 it revolutionized the electronic and computing world by replacing the unreliable valve. This
solid state device is small, reliable, cheap and

consumes very little power. It can be used as an amplifier or as a switching device, the latter forming the basis of computer **logic** and **memory** circuits. Joining two transistors together leads to **astable** and **bistable** circuits which are the building blocks of today's electronic systems. Transistors are made from p-type and n-type (n-p-n being the most common) **semiconductors** such as **silicon**, germanium and **gallium arsenide**. There are two main types of transistor, the junction transistor and the field-effect transistor (FET). The first type, sometimes known as 'bipolar', is the faster acting and more robust of the two though the voltage at which it works is more critical and a stabilized 5-volt power supply is required. The first **chip** was created in 1959 when a (junction) transistor and resistor were built together, hence the term *transistor-resistor-logic* or TRL.

tree A non-linear method of storing **data** in a computer. One piece of data relates to several other pieces and each one of these then relates to more. The computer tree, however, is upside down with the branches spreading out downwards.

For example, an alternative to storing the following seven names alphabetically would be to use a tree structure:

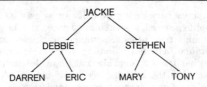

Note that MARY can be accessed from the root (JACKIE) as the third piece of data via JACKIE and STEPHEN. In fact all can be accessed within three. If the names were stored in alphabetical order MARY would be the fifth piece of data accessed.

truncation When reducing the number of significant figures in a number, truncation, unlike **rounding**, involves their removal without any consideration of their value.

For example, truncation to three significant figures of the numbers 56.79 and 23820 would result in the loss of a 9 and 2 respectively:

> 56.79 would become 56.7
> 23820 would become 23800

truth table A table usually filled with 0s and 1s to show the changes carried out by logical operations such as **AND**, **OR**, **XOR**, and **NOT**.

For example, an AND gate only gives an output of logical value 1 when all its inputs have a logical value of 1:

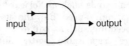

Input		Output
0	0	0
0	1	0
1	0	0
1	1	1

truth table Truth table for a two-input
AND gate.

turnkey A turnkey system for a **micro-computer** loads the required **operating system**
as soon as one switches on, and then automati-
cally loads all the necessary applications programs, thus leaving the computer in a 'ready to
use' state.

turtle A device whose movements are controlled by a computer. It may be a floor turtle
with means of propulsion along the ground or a
screen turtle that moves and draws lines on a
screen.

turtle graphics Part of an interactive **program**
such as LOGO, which allows the user to explore
spatial concepts (using design, draw, repeat etc.)
by controlling the movement of a **screen** or floor

turtle. Commands such as 'forward 40' and 'left 90' are normally used but the user can also design procedures such as 'square' and 'rectangle' which are repeatable with different size **variables**.

typeface   The particular design (**font**) or shape of the characters used by a **printer** or typewriter to put marks onto paper.

U

ultra high frequency (UHF)   A particular range of radio waves having wavelengths approximately between 10 and 100 cm. They are used for television transmissions and as **micro-computer outputs** which connect through the aerial socket for display on a television receiver. Frequency values are a few hundred million hertz.

uncommitted logic array (ULA)   A **chip** on which there are sets of **logic circuits** that have not yet been connected together. Each set is complete in itself but has to be linked to the others by one or more connections.

Thus a chip manufacturer makes his standard ULA which has the final layer (the circuit pattern) added according to the purchaser's specification. This enables the purchaser to obtain his own particular type of chip without the large expense of having one specially designed. See also **application specific integrated circuits**.

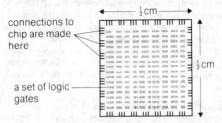

connections to chip are made here

a set of logic gates

$\frac{1}{2}$ cm

$\frac{1}{2}$ cm

uncommitted logic array

underflow   The generation of a number, e.g. by division, which is too small for the **computer** to store (the computer would store zero). In **floating-point notation** using two 8-bit **words** this would happen when the resulting number was below 10^{-39}. That is a one, divided by a one with thirty-nine noughts.

For example, on a six-digit **calculator** dividing the number 0.000001 by 2 would give zero. Underflow is the name given when the right-hand digits are lost.

UNIX An operating system developed by Bell Laboratories with the object of improving **software portability**. The **high-level language** C was designed for use with it.

update The process of changing a **file** or **program** package so as to bring it up-to-date. This would include additions of new **data**, changes in data already held and alterations to the program to remove minor errors which have been found. The latter is sometimes called a '**patch**'.

For example, an update may be necessary to a payroll package as a result of new Government legislation on PAYE (pay-as-you-earn income tax).

upgrade The improvement of a piece of **hardware**, firmware or **software**. Often an option given to the purchaser (e.g. 512 K or 640 K **memory**) which can be taken up at a later time.

user group A group of people who meet or correspond regularly because of their interest in a particular machine or suite of **programs**. Most makes of **microcomputers** have their own user groups, generally supported by the manufacturer but controlled by the members. Meetings allow the sharing of both problems and solutions and provide advance information on new products. Much is to be gained at a small cost for all those who become members.

user port A socket on the **microcomputer**'s casing which allows the user to connect additional equipment or **peripherals**. Each port may have a different pin layout according to the type of **signal** sent or received, and will probably have a **serial interface** or parallel interface incorporated, or in some cases an **analogue** to **digital** converter.

utility programs **Programs** designed to assist an operator to perform particular tasks such as listing a **file** held on magnetic tape or **disk**, or copying **data** from one disk to another prior to a program run.

V

validation A check to ensure that data is sensible and accurate, as mistakes can be made during the collection, inputting or transferring of data. Validity checks do not totally eliminate mistakes, but they make it difficult for wrong data to get through to the computer or its **peripherals**.

For numbers where checks for accuracy have to be made subsequently, there are several methods of generating a coded number that can be more readily checked. In each case a validation **program** will check the number each time it is used, by duplicating the calculation, and if this routine fails to produce the same answer then an error has been found.

hash total or *checksum*: a reference digit or number from each item in a **file** is added together to give a meaningless total, which although meaningless should stay constant.

check digit: this is an extra digit calculated from the original digits of a number, put on the end of that number and used to confirm that there has not been a change whilst being transferred either by hand or wire. This digit can be the result of a simple calculation such as dividing by a predetermined number (a **modulus**); any remainder is then used to calculate the digit that has to be appended to the original number.

weighted check digit: an extra stage of multiplying each digit of the number by a different factor is included. It is reckoned that it would be hundreds of years before a wrongly entered number got through.

Other validation routines could be:

Range checks: checks that ensure the data is within accepted limits and therefore sensible.

Example: IF age%<1 OR age%>120 THEN PRINT 'Please re-enter age'.

Checks on number tables: The use of **hash** (batch) **totals**. All the data in the table is summed to produce a nonsense total. This total is checked at the preparation and input stage.

Checks on strings (words/names/lists etc): The use of **look-up** reference **tables** which are files of data such as names, addresses, lists stored on disk. The computer compares and matches each entry against the data table.

All these validity checks can be programmed into the computer so that it can carry out automatic checking.

variable   Anything that can change or vary, but for computers it usually refers to a numerical value or a **text string** that has been defined as a variable. To enable the speedy accessing of such **data**, different programming **languages** have adopted their own methods of labelling variables. This enables the operating **system** to reserve sections of **memory** for storing variables, and then, knowing the **address** of their **location**, gives immediate access. Each variable has a name and a type to identify it.

Examples of common variable types in

BASIC:	PASCAL:
name%=integer (whole number) variable	var name: integer
name$=string or text variable	var name: char
name=real number variable (accepts decimal parts)	var name: real

Using variables:

answer%=first%+second%
PRINT carname$

This will display the contents of carname$.

DATE and TIME would both be defined and stored as variables. If data is in the form of **strings** (strings of characters), several **locations** together might be used to hold the data.

verification   This is a check that something has been accurately typed and transmitted. It is the job of the inputter to type accurately what is before them, but mistakes can be made. For example, some typical mistakes in keying in 041772 could be:

(a) Transcription error (a digit wrongly typed): 041792

(b) Transposition (a pair of digits change place): 042771

(c) Double transposition (double pairs change place): 014277

(d) Random errors (complete mess)

Verification ensures such errors do not get through as mistakes can be very serious.

Using paper methods (tape or punched cards), a second copy is keyed. If there are any differences from the first copy the reader will jam the **keyboard**. The inputter then decides which copy is the accurate one.

With magnetic media (tape or **disks**), a second copy is keyed which is also put on tape or **disk unit** and the two compared. With transmitted **data**, a check is made on **parity bit**, an extra bit added at the preparation stage for each **word**. The check will show if data has been corrupted during transmission.

very large-scale integration (VLSI) As with **large-scale integration** (LSI) this is a measure of the number of logic **gates** on a single **chip**. Between 1960 and 1970 designers produced more and more logic gates on a single chip, the number approximately doubling every year from the single gate of 1959. First came **small-scale integration** (SSI) with up to 20 logic gates and then medium-scale integration (MSI) with 20 to 100. By 1969 we had large-scale integration with 100 to 5000 logic gates and since 1975 we have had very large-scale integration with numbers above 5000 on a chip about a half-centimetre square.

video conference A discussion between two or more groups of people who are in different places but can see and hear each other. Pictures and sound are carried by the **telecommunication** network and such conferences take place across the world using satellites.

video disk See **optical disc**.

video signal The **signal** in a television set that provides the picture, although in the case of a television transmission entering through the aerial socket it has to be separated from the sound. Most **microcomputers** will display their **output** on a television set via the aerial socket though for better picture definition one should use a **monitor** which accepts a video signal (this has a lower frequency than the UHF aerial signal). Some video recorders have a composite video output and for this reason many **television receivers** are now being made with video inputs as well as UHF. For the clearest colour picture however the **red**, **green** and **blue** video signals should be sent separately and this requires both an RGB computer output and an RGB video monitor.

videotex Any information service which can

display text on the screen of a television set. The code may be transmitted as part of a television picture (teletext) or as a coded telephone signal (viewdata). A typical page has 24 lines with up to 40 characters per line.

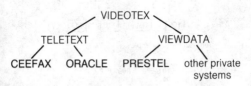

videotex The relationship between different systems.

viewdata An information retrieval service in the form of **pages** or frames which the user can call up from a **dumb terminal** or keypad. The pages are transmitted via phone lines from a central computer or direct from the IP (**information** provider). The information is a structured part of a **tree** system, each frame having definite well-defined links from the root downwards. Users can access pages by moving up or down a particular pathway from the root, through choices listed on screen and made at the keypad.

Some viewdata services now allow interaction (two-way communication) with users, thus allowing the development of teleshopping, telebanking and booking services.

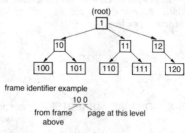

frame identifier example

100 0
from frame   page at this level
above

viewdata

virtual memory A facility available in large modern computers whereby the **programmer** is not restricted by the size of the machine's **memory**. The machine translates virtual **locations** that the programmer has specified into actual locations as and when required using **backing stores** to provide the extra memory space.

virus A routine introduced into a **program** that, when activated, produces unwanted results that can range from displaying messages on the screen to the partial or total corruption of programs and **data**. So called because the 'infection' can spread from one **disk** to another, even across machines. The virus orginates from someone wishing to cause problems, who gains access to the system directly or via a disk.

visual display unit (VDU) A device, like a television set, used to display the **output** from a computer. It is very similar to a **monitor** except that it is usually associated with a **keyboard** and is often used as a **terminal** to a computer sometimes from a distance.

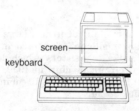

screen

keyboard

visual display unit

voice input **Data** or commands entered by the spoken word instead of with a **keyboard** or other device. This can only be done with equipment using **speech recognition** techniques, and apart from its computer applications, it is also used in the operating of a variety of mechanical, electrical or electronic devices. At the present machines are able to accept a range of words, but these do have to be spoken clearly.

volatile memory All types of memory which lose their stored **data** as soon as the power is switched off.

For example, **core store** and **RAM chips** are volatile whereas magnetic **disk**, **optical disc** and **bubble memory** are not.

W

wafer A thin slice cut from a large crystal of germanium or **silicon**. First used in the mid-1950s to make **transistors** which led to the **integrated circuit** or **chip** in 1959. A typical **wafer** would be 0.01 in thick, 10 cm in diameter and contain 250 chips.

wand Another name for a **light pen**.

weighted check digit A method of validating **data** entry, where this digit is put at the end of a number or **string** of characters to confirm that there has not been a change whilst being transferred either by hand or wire.

For example, consider the ISBN number of this book; the last digit is in fact a check digit.

0 00 459250 6

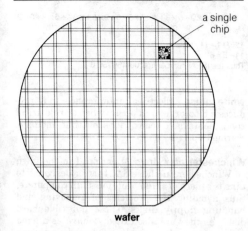

a single chip

wafer

0 gives the country (0 England, 2 Germany),
00 is the publisher (Collins being the first),
459 is used by Collins for the department code,
250 is used by Collins for the list number within
the department,
6 is the check digit calculated from the previous
nine digits by multiplying the first by 10, the
next by 9 and so on, then adding up the totals,
dividing by 11 and subtracting the remainder
from 11.

$0×10+0×9+0×8+4×7+5×6+9×5+2×4+5×3+0×2$
$=\ 0\ \ +\ 0\ \ +\ 0\ \ +\ 28\ +\ 30\ +\ 45\ +\ 8\ +\ 15\ +\ 0$

$126/11=11$ remainder 5

$11-5=6$

Thus the ISBN number is 0 00 459250 6

white noise Electrical interference that produces a buzz or hum. It occurs when the electrical components have been on for some time and have warmed up.

Winchester disk drive Developed in the town of Winchester in the USA, this is designed to take the place of a **disk unit** for small computers, thus avoiding the problems of removing and handling **floppy disks**. These inflexible hard disks, as they are also called, behave as a fixed disk system with the read/write head being much closer to the disk. In this way the tracks are much closer together and far more data can be stored.

For example: a 5.25-inch Winchester disk could hold a hundred times as much as a normal floppy disk. It would also rotate about 10 times faster.

Sizes currently available include 5.25 inches, 8 inches and 14 inches. Many **microcomputer** manufacturers offer a choice of **Winchester** or floppy **disk drives** with the same machine.

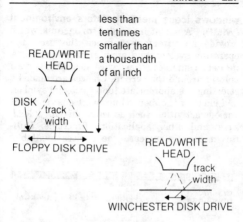

less than ten times smaller than a thousandth of an inch

READ/WRITE HEAD

DISK / track width

FLOPPY DISK DRIVE

READ/WRITE HEAD / track width

WINCHESTER DISK DRIVE

Winchester disk drive Comparison with a floppy disk drive.

window An area on a computer **screen** which is showing a particular display. Within a **software** package there may be a **text** window describing the picture in a graphic window. Within a **word processor** different windows may simultaneously show different **files** or different parts of the same file. Alternatively different windows may show different applications.

windows icons menus pointers environment (WIMP) A set of integrated **programs** which provide an **interface** between the user, the operating system, and application programs. A **mouse**, a small desktop device, is used to move a pointer around the **screen**. Choices are made by selecting the appropriate **icon** (pictorial symbol) and clicking the mouse buttons. Icons represent various activities, such as scrap, directory, load, save, and other applications functions. **Pull-down menus** increase the choices available.

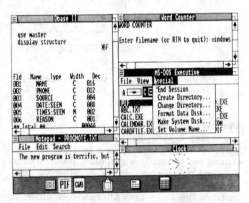

WIMP   An example of a WIMP screen.

Several screen **windows** can be displayed, allowing enlargement or reduction within the overall screen-size limits. The WIMP environment largely makes the **keyboard** redundant for issuing instructions.

Some WIMP programs can allow multi-tasking, whereby several programs can be in **memory** and you can switch between them by using the mouse. A program can be used whilst a previous one is being processed. (The computer processes a bit of each at a time, but with today's powerful **microprocessors**, the speed reduction is hardly noticeable.)

Popular WIMP environments include GEM and Microsoft Windows. Many CAD, WP, **graphics** and **desktop publishing** applications include WIMP features.

word The set of **binary digits** that fill one **location** in a computer's **memory**, and hence the maximum number that can be treated by the computer as a single unit for processing and parallel transmission. 8-bit words require 8 wires; 16-bit words require 16 wires and so on. The length of a word depends on the particular computer but is made up of **bytes** which in turn are made up of bits. The longer the word the more quickly the CPU can work, but longer words require more complex **integrated circuits**.

Most instructions that operate the processor contain two parts, an operator (add, subtract) and an **operand** containing the address of the memory location to be used. Using a 24-bit word this might be arranged in 8 and 16 bits and could occupy one location in a 24-bit computer:

★ ★ ★ ★ ★ ★ ★ ★	★ ★ ★ ★ ★ ★ ★ ★ ★ ★ ★ ★ ★ ★ ★ ★

8 BITS	16 BITS
operator	operand
0–255	0–65535

or three memory locations in an 8-bit word machine:

Some CPUs can process double words (i.e. treating two words as a single unit to speed up operations) whilst others can cope with *variable word length processing* where the word length is varied according to the type of **data** being stored.

word processor This is a computer specifically used for the typing and production of letters, reports and documents. In addition to allowing corrections of a single **character**, or a phrase, it will **justify** both left and right margins, centralize headings, move paragraphs, number pages, search for particular words and check spellings. In some cases it will do mathematical calculations, column moves, automatically update figures taken from a changing **database** and offer the user a Thesaurus. Wordwrap (automatic word fit between margins) can be used, and as well as justifying text after insertions, **font** and print sizes can be altered.

Modern word-processing has WYSIWIG (pronounced wiziwig and meaning What You See Is

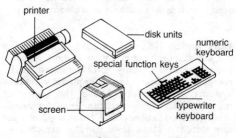

word processor

What You Get) **screen** features in that text on screen is displayed exactly as it will look when printed on paper.

Some manufacturers offer specially designed machines dedicated solely for use as word processors, and these often have extra keys to take the place of **commands** and functions; others offer word processing packages for use with particular computers. Word processors can be **mouse**-driven instead of being controlled totally from a **keyboard**, and although there are variations between the different word processors (the number of extra keys, for example) the quality of the final document depends on the type of **printer**. Modern technology could replace the printer with **electronic mail** whereby the text created on one word processor is sent via the telephone system to another office where it is read from a screen and/or stored electronically.

work station In today's modern office one sits not just at a desk but at a work station. This has its own **visual display unit** connected to the company's **database** as well as public **viewdata** systems. A **keyboard** allows the typing of memos and letters which can be sent immediately via the telephone line. Incoming messages are stored so that they can be accepted as required. With such developments the work station does not need to be in an office; it could be on the factory floor or at home.

wrap To break a line of text which is too long for the **screen** or **printer**. It is broken at the right hand edge and automatically carried over to the next line. Similarly after the bottom line of the text on a screen the next line appears, at the top, overwriting the first line, though **scroll** is an alternative to this.

X

xerographic laser printer See **laser printer**.

X-ray lithography The proccess of using X-rays to etch circuit lines of about a tenth of a micron (1 micron = 1 millionth of a metre) onto **thin film memories**. Using such methods it should be possible to increase to 4 billion the number of components on a single **chip**.

X-Y The two directions of the **computer screen** or **printer output**. X represents the horizontal direction and Y the vertical. See also **plotter**.

Y

yell What one does when things go wrong. One problem for the **microcomputer** user occurs when the **backing store** (**tape** or **disk**) becomes corrupt in some way and it is not possible to load a particular **program**. It is at this point that the user realizes that a **back-up** copy was never made let alone the third copy recommended as good practice. Most companies that use a computer are often unaware of how dependent their business becomes on the machine. In fact if their computer system was put out of action completely most would find it difficult to survive. Hence the need for adequate insurance and back-up facilities.

Z

zero-fill The replacement of a set of **characters** by zeros. Often used to fill a location ready for the later transfer of data so that it is not affected by previous stored values.

zone Specific regions on a **punched card** or print positions on **screen** or paper.

For example, in **BASIC**, variables separated by semi-colons are printed together whilst those separated by commas are printed in separate zones.

a punched card

zone

zone refining The method used to obtain a pure substance such as the **silicon** required for making **integrated circuits**. Starting at one end the material is melted and this molten zone is made to move along the sample to the other end. This is repeated several times always in the same direction and each time more of the impurities move with the molten zone to one end of the sample. In the case of silicon this pure substance is doped and then grown into a large cylindrical crystal (using a **seed crystal**) from which **wafers** are sliced.

ABBREVIATIONS AND ACRONYMS

Bold type indicates that a more comprehensive entry may be found under the heading in the main text.

A

A/D	Analogue to Digital
ADA	A high-level programming language
ADC	**Analogue-digital converter**
ADP	Automatic Data Processing
AFIPS	American Federation of Information Processing Societies
AI	**Artificial Intelligence**
ALGOL	ALGOrithmic Language
ALU	**Arithmetic Logic Unit**
AND	A Logic Gate
APL	A Programming Language
ASCII	American Standard Code for Information Interchange
ASICS	**Application Specific Integrated Circuits**
ATM	**Automated Teller Machine**

B

BABT	British Approvals Board of Telecommunications
BASIC	Beginner's All-purpose Symbolic Instruction Code
BCD	**Binary Coded Decimal**
BCS	British Computer Society
BIT	**BInary DigiT**
BLAISE	British Library Automated Information Service
bps	Bits Per Second
BSI	**British Standards Institute**

C

C	A high-level programming language
CAA	Computer-Aided Administration
CAD	Computer-Aided Design
CAFS	**Contents Addressable File Store**
CAI	Common Air Interface
CAL	**Computer Assisted Learning**
CAM	Computer-Aided Manufacture
CBL	Computer-Based Learning
CBT	**Computer-Based Training**

CCITT	Consultative Committee International Telegraph and Telephone
CEG	Computer Education Group
CISC	**Complex Instruction Set Computer**
CD-I	**Compact Disc Interactive**
CD-Rom	**Compact Disc** Read Only Memory
CD-Rom XA	Compact Disc Read Only Memory with extended architecture
CIM	Computer Integrated Manufacture
CM	Central Memory
CML	**Computer Managed Learning**
CMOS	Complementary Metal Oxide Semiconductor
CNC	Computer Numeric Control
COBOL	Common Business Oriented Language
COM	Computer Output on Microfilm
COMMS	**Communications**
COMAL	COMmon Algorithmic Language
CORAL	COmmon Real-time Application Language
CP/M	Control Program for Microcomputers

cps	Characters Per Second
CPU	**Central Processing Unit**
CUG	Closed User Group

D

D/A	Digital to Analogue
DOS	**Disk Operating System**
DP	**Data Processing**
DTL	Diode Transistor Logic
DTP	**Desk Top Publishing**
DVI	Digital Video Interactive

E

EAROM	Electrically Alterable ROM
EBCDIC	Extended Binary Coded Decimal Interchange Code
ECCTIS	Educational Counselling and Credit Transfer Information Service
ECMA	European Computer Manufacturers' Association
EDI	**Electronic Data Interchange**
EDP	Electronic Data Processing
EFTPOS	**Electronic Funds Transfer at Point Of Sale**
EISA	Extended Industry Standard Architecture
ELSI	Extra Large Scale Integration

EMS	Expanded Memory Specification
EPROM	Erasable Programmable Read Only Memory

F

FAX	**Facsimile**
FDDI	Fibre Distributed Data Interface
FET	Field Effect Transistor
FIFO	First in/First out
FM	Frequency Modulation
FORTRAN	FORmula TRANslation
4GL	**Fourth Generation Language**

G H

GIGO	**Garbage** In Garbage Out
GByte	**Gigabyte (1000 megabytes)**
GUI	**Graphical User Interface**
HEX	**Hexadecimal notation**
Hz	Hertz

I

IAL	International Algebraic Language
IAR	**Instruction Address Register**
IAS	**Immediate Access Store**

IBM	International Business Machines
IC	**Integrated Circuit**
ICL	International Computers Limited
IEE	Institute of Electrical Engineers
IEEE	Institute of Electronic and Electrical Engineers (USA)
IFIP	International Federation for Information Processing
INTELSAT	INternational TELecommunications SATellite consortium
I/O	Input and **Output**
IP	Information Provider
IPDS	International Packet Data Service
IPSS	International Packet Switch Stream
ISBN	International Standard Book Number
ISDN	**Integrated Services Digital Network**
ISO	International Standards Organisation
IT	**Information Technology**
IV	**Interactive Video**

J K

JCL	**Job Control Language**
K	Kilo
KBS	Knowledge Based Systems
KByte	**Kilobyte**

L

LAN	**Local Area Network**
LCD	**Liquid Crystal Display**
LED	**Light Emitting Diode**
LOGO	A high-level language
lpm	Lines Per Minute
LSI	**Large Scale Integration**

M

MAP	Microprocessor Application Project
MByte	**Megabyte**
MCA	Micro Channel Architecture
MICR	**Magnetic Ink** Character Recognition
MIDI	**Musical Instrument Digital Interface**
mips	Million Instructions per Second
MIS	Management Information Systems

MISP	Microelectronics Industry Support Programme
MODEM	MOdulator-DEModulator
MPU	**Microprocessor** Unit
MS-DOS	Microsoft Disk Operating System
MSI	Medium Scale Integration

N O

NAND	A "Not AND" Logic Gate
NCC	National Computing Centre/ National Curriculum Council
NCET	National Council for Educational Technology
NEQ	**Non-Equivalence Logic Gate**
NERIS	National Educational Resources Information Service
NLQ	Near Letter Quality
NOR	A "Not OR" Logic Gate
NOT	A Logic Gate
NTSC	National Television Standard Committee
NUA	Network User Address
NUI	Network User Identity
OA	Office Automation
OCR	**Optical Character Recognition**
ODA	**Open Document Architecture**

oem	Original Equipment Manufacturer
OMR	Optical Mark Reader
OP-CODE	**Operation Code**
OR	A Logic Gate
OSI	**Open Systems Interconnect**
OS/2	A disk operating system

P

PAD	Packet Assembler/Disassembler
PAL	Phase Alternation Line (A colour TV system)
PASCAL	High-level programming language
PC	**Personal Computer**
PCB	**Printed Circuit Board**
PC-DOS	Personal Computer Disk Operating System
PICK	An operating system
PIXEL	PICture ELements
PILOT	An author language
PIN	Personal Identification Number
PIO	Programmable Input/Output
PL/1	Programming Language 1
PLATO	A CBL system
POS	**Point of Scale (terminal)**
PROLOG	PROgramming in LOGic

PROM	**Programmable Read Only Memory**
PSS	**Packet Switch Stream**
PSTN	Public Switched Telephone Network

Q R

QWERTY	The normal typewriter keyboard
RAM	**Random Access Memory**
RF	Radio Frequency
RGB	**Red, Green, Blue**
RISC	**Reduced Instruction Set Computer**
RJE	Remote Job Entry
ROM	**Read Only Memory**
RS232	A standard serial interface
RS423	A standard serial interface

S T

SECAM	Systeme En Couleurs A Mémoire (a colour TV system)
SPOOL	Simultaneous Peripheral Operation On-Line
SSI	**Small Scale Integration**
2GL	**Second Generation language**
TByte	**Tetrabyte (1000 gigabytes)**
TRL	Transistor-Resistor-Logic

TSR	Terminate and Stay Resident
TTL	Transistor Transistor Logic
3GL	**Third Generation language**

U

UHF	**Ultra High Frequency**
ULA	**Uncommitted Logic Array**
UNIVAC	UNIVersal Automatic Computer
UNIX	An operating system

V

V21	A standard protocol for **MODEM**s (also others like V22, V23)
V24	A standard serial interface used in Europe and other non-N America areas.
VDU	**Visual Display Unit**
VHF	Very High Frequency
VLF	Very Low Frequency
VLSI	**Very Large Scale Integration**

W

| WAN | Wide Area Network |
| WIMP | **Windows, Icons, Menus, Pointers** |

WORM	Write Once Read Many (times)
WP	**Word Processor**
WYSIWYG	What You See Is What You Get

X

X-Y	Two directions at right angles
X400	A telecommunication standard
XOR	**Exclusive-OR-logic gate**

From page 101:

Pitch   (1) A tar substance often used on the hulls of boats to inhibit growth and thus make them go fast.
(2) To throw something.
(3) A cricket or football ground.
(4) The spacing of characters in a line of text.
(5) Part of the description of a musical note.

Fast   (1) To travel at high speed.
(2) To 'make fast' a boat is to tie it up so that it cannot move at any speed.
(3) To go without food.
(4) Strong against attack.
(5) Lasting, as in a 'fast colour', i.e. does not wash out.